1978

W9-CLF-738

THE HOUSE, THE CITY, AND THE JUDGE

Essay and Monograph Series
of The Liberal Arts Press

OSKAR PIEST, FOUNDER

ATHENA CASTING HER VOTE FOR ORESTES

The Corsini Vase. Roman copy, or compilation, of Greek
elements from the late fifth and early fourth centuries.

THE HOUSE, THE CITY, AND THE JUDGE

The Growth of Moral
Awareness in the
ORESTEIA

RICHARD KUHNS

Associate Professor of Philosophy,
Columbia University

THE **BOBBS-MERRILL** COMPANY, INC.
A SUBSIDIARY OF HOWARD W. SAMS & CO., INC.
Publishers • INDIANAPOLIS • NEW YORK

Library of Congress Catalog No. 61-18061

Copyright © 1962 by The Bobbs-Merrill Company, Inc.
Printed in the United States of America
First Edition

PREFACE

The following essay, begun out of curiosity about the *Oresteia*, unites literary and philosophical methods in the exploration of its subject. While I began with a belief in the serious philosophical concerns of the greatest literature, I became convinced as this study developed that what stands as criticism in the arts requires a broad foundation in the problems and perspectives of philosophy. This inquiry is therefore offered to both philosophers and critics in the hope that they will be sympathetic, on the one hand to a literary work read as serious in philosophic content, and on the other to philosophy nourished by literature. I believe the distinctions we have facilely made between the didactic and the literary were not accepted in antiquity, and that we have found them meaningful only through a pervasive disillusionment about the power of literary statements in the face of the impressive claims to truth of science.

Literature has more than a mimetic interest in truth; one of the primary values of literature is truth, although it is by no means the only value. That the Athenian world took the literary seriously is evident from the arguments which, if Plato is to be trusted, received so much attention at the dinner table and in the market place. The question was, who could legitimately claim to know the truth. The dramatist was one of the chief contenders; perhaps in the popular mind he was the only successful one since the playwright was most influential in proposing and challenging ideas to the citizenry. And of these Aeschylus stands out in both his profundity of thought and scope of literary genius. Of his few surviving plays, the *Oresteia* stands out as most wise in the fullness and acuity of its political investigation. Perhaps the political—by which I mean the moral foundations and instrumentations of men living in groups—is most fully explored by means of the drama, because here the central concern is human action, and it is that which serious considerations of the political can never lose sight of.

In any case, the *Oresteia*, by being placed in the tradition of classical political thought, contributes to our understanding of the political, and itself becomes more intelligible as its action is explored with the help of that thought.

For better or worse, the work of art which Athens of the fifth and fourth centuries knew has become a drama altered from its original. But from the aesthetic point of view, the aesthetic object we know, no matter how it has suffered in its derivation from the original, is a legitimate, and in fact the only, representation we can have. I have accepted the version presented by the very powerful translation of Richmond Lattimore. Indeed, he takes liberties with the text as we know it, but I believe they are justified in most cases by the ambiguity of the language and the difficulties of interpretation. Where Lattimore's readings appear dubious or vague I point out my difficulty with them, or try to give a more literal interpretation. By and large his reading is dramatically coherent, explicit in interpretation, and adequate to the re-establishment of the text as a drama of remarkable subtlety and design. Certainly the work is to be known in this rendering by many students; as such it merits close attention, and in part it is their needs which have led me to write this essay.

I have discussed my work with several friends from whom I have learned a great deal and by whom I have been saved from serious error. The thanks here expressed to them does not imply that they are in agreement with my conclusions. In fact, we disagree on certain points, but where there is merit in this study it is due in large measure to their suggestions and their eagerness to argue the issues with me. In particular I wish to thank George and Barbara Tovey of Mt. Holyoke College for their careful reading of the manuscript and their thoughtful criticisms; their sympathetic understanding of classical philosophy has been of the greatest benefit to me. John Stewart of Dartmouth College has given me the benefit of his meticulous criticism and encouraging enthusiasm. Martin Ostwald of Swarthmore College has made helpful suggestions on many problems of interpretation. My colleague, James Walsh, has helped me to see the moral issues more clearly, and has pointed out several ways in which the arguments about responsibility relate to contemporary ethical problems. I am deeply grateful to the Columbia University Council for Research in the Social Sciences for a publication subsidy. The realization of this book has been immeasurably helped by Oskar Piest, who, through a distinguished career as publisher and editor, has contributed so many works to the enrichment of humanistic studies.

My debt to scholars in the classics is, as the notes and bibliography indicate, immense. Often I can only restate their conclusions, or let them speak for themselves. I hope I have been able to contribute to their work by joining their arguments to a broader point of view than has traditionally been assumed in regard to the *Oresteia*. My intention has been to fit the drama, with its philosophical, religious, and political content, within a comprehensive network of ideas that are peculiar to the Athenian thinkers of the Hellenic age, and at the same time especially suggestive to us today. This aim has necessitated an exposition that spreads as it moves along, so that what begins as detailed reference to the action of the drama, presented in brief factual chapters, ends as an exhibition of a variegated fabric of concepts and beliefs, no longer directly a part of the drama, but, as it were, its ultimate towardness in the realm of philosophical speculation.

R. K.

ACKNOWLEDGMENTS

The author acknowledges with gratitude permission to quote material from the following sources:

Aeschylus, *Oresteia*, from *The Complete Greek Tragedies*, ed. David Grene and Richmond Lattimore. Copyright 1953, the University of Chicago Press. Reprinted by permission of the publishers.

Aristotle, *Metaphysics*, tr. Richard Hope. Copyright 1952, Columbia University Press. Reprinted by permission of the publishers.

Committee of the Classical Instructors of Harvard University (editors), *Harvard Studies in Classical Philosophy*, XLIX (Cambridge, Mass.: Harvard University Press, 1938). Reprinted by permission of the publishers.

G. F. Else, *Aristotle's Poetics: The Argument*. Copyright 1957, Harvard University Press. Reprinted by permission of the publishers.

Georges Méautis, *L'Oedipe à Colone et le culte des héros* (Paris, 1936), reprinted by permission of the University of Neuchâtel.

R. B. Onions, *The Origin of European Thought* (Cambridge, England, 1954), reprinted by permission of the Cambridge University Press.

E. T. Owen, *The Harmony of Aeschylus* (Toronto, 1952), reprinted by permission of Clarke, Irwin and Company.

E. P. Papanoutsos, *La catharsis des passions d'après Aristote* (Athens, 1953), reprinted by permission of L'Institut Français d'Athènes.

Plato, *Laws*, Vol. II, tr. R. G. Bury (Cambridge, Mass.: Harvard University Press, 1926), reprinted by permission of the publishers.

L. A. Post, *Homer to Menander* (Berkeley, 1951), reprinted by permission of the University of California Press.

H. J. Rose, "Theology and Mythology in Aeschylus," *Harvard Theological Review*, XXXIX (1946), reprinted by permission of the Harvard Divinity School.

Friedrich Solmsen, *Hesiod and Aeschylus* (Ithaca, 1949), reprinted by permission of the Cornell University Press.

CONTENTS

CONTENTS

THE HOUSE, THE CITY, AND THE JUDGE

To M.P.K.

They purify themselves by staining themselves with other blood, as if one were to step into mud in order to wash off mud. But a man would be thought mad if any of his fellow-men should perceive him acting thus. Moreover, they talk to these statues (of theirs) as if one were to hold conversation with houses, in his ignorance of the nature of both gods and heroes.

(Heraclitus. Diels, Frag. 5, tr. K. Freeman)

Surely, the drive of a god is behind him, to bring law to the lawless people.

(Bacchylides, *The Coming of Theseus*, tr. Richmond Lattimore)

CHAPTER ONE

INTRODUCTION

The undiminished significance of our legacy from the Hellenic world accounts for the astonishing accumulation of interpretations and commentaries upon a rather meager body of literature. Among these remains, Greek tragic drama has indeed been accorded its share of scrutiny. Despite changes in opinion about what constitutes a "proper" dramatic situation (and from time to time Greek drama has been declared incapable of achieving that excellence) the religious and philosophical content of Greek tragedy remains forever provocative and enlightening. Preferences for certain classical plays over others have been stated on the ground of dramatic intensity, tight-knit action, and portrayal of character; but beyond that, a need to understand Greek culture has led again and again to a study of its drama as a whole, because there we have found an artistic presentation of Greek self-consciousness.

In giving satisfaction to both dramatic and intellectual requirements no tragic drama has been more successful than the *Oresteia* by Aeschylus. This trilogy is composed of an opening drama sufficiently violent to satisfy our love of spectacle, and of two concluding dramas which, though rarely played because of their difficult action, have provided an intellectual challenge to literary critics of every generation. Our modern predilection for intensity has led to a concentration upon the *Agamemnon* rather than the *Libation Bearers* and the *Eumenides*. But the central character of the *Oresteia,* as the title makes clear, is Orestes; it is his action which ties the three plays together into a meaningful work of art. Even though that action may prove disappointing to us as "theater," it is a type of human action which, from the point of view of a Greek audience, merits the most sympathetic observation, for it is the action of a man coming to moral awareness. It is, most inclusively, the representation of what it is to know the true nature of gods and heroes.

5

Dramatic subject matter of this kind is aesthetically and philosophically foreign to contemporary theater since the action and the conclusion are an explanation of and a statement about the nature of the cosmos. Aeschylus' trilogy is fundamentally philosophical in its concerns and its thought. It does not compete with or take the place of philosophy, for it is a work of art. Yet, as we will see, in its own time and in the minds of those it inspired it is to be considered far more theoretical than we, with our distinction between the scientific and poetic uses of language, are able to admit. Thus conceived, the *Oresteia* is more than the story of the murder of Agamemnon, the vengeance of Orestes, and his ultimate acquittal. It is concerned to reflect the development of moral awareness not simply in the individual, but in a whole people who have come to an enlarged understanding of the universe they inhabit.[1]

That the serious content of the work has been recognized is evident from the uses to which it has been put. It has frequently been used to provide factual evidence for a great variety of hypotheses in cultural history. It has been assumed to be an expression of personal views held by Aeschylus; the statement of theological doctrines maintained by the more reflective Athenian citizens; the record of ritualistic practices of purification; and a partially reliable historical account of a development from one kind of social organization to another which occurred long before Aeschylus wrote. It has been declared to be anthropologically both sound and false, serious throughout, and in part serious, in

---

[1] There has been much debate over the question whether or not Greek drama exhibits character development as we have come to know it in the drama of the Elizabethan and modern tradition. While many of the characters in the *Oresteia* are simply revealed as persons of a certain kind, I believe there is an effort to depict Orestes as one who has changed and who does change during the course of the action. This is effected by means of the drama as a whole, not only by the speeches of Orestes. The play can be viewed as both an exhibit of and a commentary upon a character who is changing. Bruno Snell maintains that "Aeschylus is at great pains to represent the characters in his tragedies as independent agents, acting upon the bidding of their own hearts, instead of merely reacting to external stimuli." I am in full agreement with this. (*The Discovery of the Mind* [Cambridge, Mass., 1953], pp. 103-4.)

part facetious. The arguments which occur in it, particularly in the concluding trial scene, have been taken by some critics as mere entertainment for an audience delighting in forensic contest, and have been taken by others as an expression of profound moral truths.[2]

In the variety of uses and interpretations the dramatic unity and meaning of the whole have quite often been lost, or declared too removed from the modern point of view for comprehension in a dramatic context. Yet there is every reason to see the trilogy as possessing remarkable dramatic integrity, as artistically sound and whole. To appreciate the work as it was intended to be in its own day and as it still can be today, the dramatic action must be understood, the religious and philosophical statements which comprise a good part of it must be made intelligible, and the relationship of the three plays must be established.

Rarely, if ever, in dramatic literature has so comprehensive a theme as Aeschylus' been attempted and realized in the theater. The development of moral awareness in a cosmic setting is usually the subject matter for philosophy. But in literature there are poetic works philosophical in their concerns. The poetic treatment of philosophical themes is the more profound, perhaps, for its assumption of defensible values which can be taken for granted only before skepticism and doubt have been given systematic philosophical expression. While the poet celebrates moral achievement, the philosopher frequently questions it. The poet senses in the individual's awareness what the philosopher or historian may chronicle in the stages of human thought and society as a whole. Thus the poet can present in the action of an individual what the philosopher and historian portray in the panorama of civilization itself. One means at the poet's disposal to achieve this presentation is myth. The poet enlarges the potentialities of myth, while the philosopher consciously moves beyond myth to conceptualization.

Today many philosophers find the mythological approach to moral questions absurd; but this is not the case in the philosophi-

[2] See Bibliography for references to the many interpretations of the *Oresteia*.

cal speculations of one of Aeschylus' fellow Athenians who shares
the dramatist's moral interests and profound belief in myth as a
revelation of significant truths. Plato is more self-conscious and
systematic in his use of myth than Aeschylus, but a comparison of
their concerns with myth will be helpful in coming to a full understanding of the *Oresteia*. Both find in myth a lesson for the
present, a penetrating commentary on the past, a revelation of
fundamental human beliefs about men and gods, and an economy
of statement that makes possible intelligible presentation of complex ideas on several levels. In both, the depths of mythical nar-
rative are unfolded and made explicit; in both, myth provides
the foundation for reflections on the family, the city, and the law.

Aeschylus' reflection on moral awareness is exhibited dramatically through the ancient story of the house of Atreus. Related
tales of the fall of prehistoric cities, the terror of blood revenge,
the intervention of gods in the actions of men are woven together
into a grand dramatic design. The wisdom of myth is made coherent with the wisdom of the society known by the poet. In the
art of Aeschylus cities, gods, heroes, and men, ancient blood morality and legalistic judgment are discovered to be interrelated, all
of a piece in a dramatic action which moves from the most remote
past to the achievement of the present.

In the *Oresteia* the central figure of Orestes makes the conjunction of present with past possible, for in that one character the
fullness of developing civilization is compacted. The growth of
moral awareness in the action of Orestes, furthered by the gods, is
in fact the consciousness of morality in the flowering of civilization as the Greeks viewed it. That awareness, presented by a tragic
poet of Aeschylus' stature, requires a drama of great complexity,
though his is marvelously economical in dramatic means. Aeschylus has left a work which is as difficult for us to understand as were
the myths he himself interpreted for the Athenians of his day. In
order to understand his poetic interpretation of myth, we in our
turn must unravel a great deal. The purpose of this essay is to unravel and reweave the themes in the *Oresteia*.

In one of the epigrammatic fragments which has come down to
us it is said that the Fates weave the immense and inescapable cun-

ning of all manner of counsels.[3] Only in the living of our lives do we discover the design they have wrought. In similar manner Aeschylus has woven counsels of remarkable complexity; and he has invoked the aid of Athena, the weaver as statesman, to weave a design for the city of men. Taking each strand in turn and following out its contribution to the whole we may apprehend the design as Aeschylus constructed it. We can invoke the aid of one who has made explicit the weaving skill required of the statesman; Plato can provide some guidance as the design is reconstituted. It will be argued that the late Platonic dialogues, particularly the *Laws,* can help us to understand parts of the *Oresteia,* for there is a common set of problems and commitments which inspire Aeschylus' drama and later Hellenic philosophy. Many of the moral issues exhibited by dramatists are analyzed by philosophers. Plato and Aristotle inherited a wisdom of myth and drama which they enlarged through conceptual analysis. The very intimate relationship of literary art and philosophy, no matter how attenuated it has become in a segment of our own humanistic inquiries, can be discovered in the time when philosophy was born.

Confirmation of this requires, first, a willingness to be serious, to give every part of the evidence a fair hearing. The figure of Orestes should be taken as the central one, for only thus can unity be restored to a work which has suffered from disproportionate attention accorded one part within it. Further, it is necessary to take the deities seriously, to understand the meanings they bear in myth and in the dramatic transmutation of myth. Finally, the significance to the drama of the family, the city, and the concept of law must be determined. Orestes' achievement is possible only under the most comprehensive conditions; they include an enlarged consciousness of both human nature and the cosmos.

The consequence of setting the manifest plot of the *Oresteia* in the universe of which it is a part is to see the human situation with greater clarity. For (and of this Aeschylus is certain) only when men understand the entire order of which they are a part can they understand themselves. Thus the conclusion of the *Oresteia* is much more than a declaration of just judgment for Orestes;

[3] *Epigrammata Graeca* 153, 3f., pp. 53-54 (ed. Kaibel).

it is a statement of the conditions under which moral and ritual pollution and cleansing exist. In short, the *Oresteia* is a drama of heavenly justice and human justice; but to see why this is so, it is necessary to consider Aeschylean (and to some extent the Greek) understanding of art as essentially an instrument of moral instruction. It is in serious drama that the circumstances responsible for human culpability and the ways of dealing with them can best be exhibited, for the dramatic statement is at once an assertion of moral truths and an effective influence in action since the experience of witnessing serious drama not only leads the audience to see things as they are, but to entertain constructive attitudes toward the human situation.

Aristotle claimed that serious drama effects catharsis, but difficulties have attended the interpretation of this assertion. The action of Orestes, when its implications are understood, will help to clarify the concept of catharsis and the view that the function of art is essentially moral, an assumption that Aeschylus shared with Plato and Aristotle.

Both ingenious and thorough explanations of catharsis have been offered in the dramatic criticism so robustly generated by Aristotle, but we still wonder about the import of this concept to the *Poetics* and to our response to serious drama. The action of the *Oresteia*, when its nature and implications are understood, will help us, I believe, to clarify the concept of catharsis as well as the belief of the Athenians that the function of art is essentially moral. The *Oresteia* can help us to understand those philosophical reconstructions of art which remain the foundation of all subsequent philosophies of art; and philosophy can help us to understand the problems which excited the art of Aeschylus.

CHAPTER TWO

THE PLOT AND THE HERO: ACTION PAST AND PRESENT

The events which make up the plot of the *Oresteia* are well known. In their fundamental order they tell the story of Agamemnon's return from the Trojan war; of his death at the hands of his wife, Clytemnestra; of his kingly power exercised by her and usurped by her lover, Aegisthus.[1] Some time later Orestes, Agamemnon's son, returns disguised, avenges his father's death by killing Clytemnestra and Aegisthus as he had been commanded to do by Apollo. He is pursued by the Erinyes, and is driven to seek help from Apollo who in turn sends him to Athens where a trial is held to determine his guilt. His case is argued by Apollo against the claims of the Erinyes. The Athenian Areopagus, assembled for the trial, votes, but is equally divided on his guilt. The case is settled by Athena who votes to acquit Orestes and then persuades the Erinyes to turn from their traditional vengeful mission to a life of protective watchfulness over the city.

To consider the trilogy in such blunt terms obscures the dramatic logic of its development and conceals the most important elements behind the retelling of a myth. To understand the *Oresteia* properly the often-told story of the house of Atreus must be

[1] It is not always understood that Agamemnon's wife ruled by right during his absence. Only Aegisthus, insofar as he undertook to rule Argos, can be called a usurper. Eduard Fraenkel comments on Clytemnestra's position as follows: "With a metaphorical use of the terms appropriate to inheritance, the poet describes things as though during the king's absence the sovereignty had passed by some ἀγχιστεία—of a peculiar sort, it must be admitted—to the queen. Neither here (lines 256ff.) nor farther on in this play are we given any unnecessary picture of the constitutional position, but so much at least is clear that Clytemnestra exercises a power which may be termed regency. This conception is in keeping with certain hints, faint though they are, in Homer." Presumably Fraenkel has in mind the position of Penelope. (*Aeschylus Agamemnon* [Oxford, 1950], II, 145.)

seen in its contribution to the theme of moral awareness in the individual. Secondly, the plot must be set in the cosmos of which it is but one event. For the *Oresteia* is the story of gods, of men, of houses, and of cities. The principal characters are not only Agamemnon, Clytemnestra, Orestes, Apollo, and Athena, but also several of the gods who do not appear yet stand behind the perceived events; cities of a noble past, like Troy; individuals, like Ixion and Asclepius who suffered at the hands of Zeus. The members of the house of Atreus have their own prototypes in a mythological past more ancient than the myth which is revitalized in the Aeschylean trilogy. And the city of Athens, raised to eminence at the conclusion of the drama, is but one of a lineage of cities less fortunate than itself. So too the gods within the play are descendants of older gods who viewed the realms of heaven and earth, the immortal and the mortal, with a different eye.

The story of Orestes, too, is not without similarity to myths more ancient than the one selected by Aeschylus for his drama. In fact, throughout the telling of the story there is a feeling on the part of all the characters that what is befalling them has happened before. The house of Atreus has been visited by terrible crimes—the cause, in fact, of present misfortune—and Orestes, as a son of the house, finds his suffering prefigured not only in the fate of his ancestors, but in the trials of heroes of old. Clytemnestra's unfaithfulness to her husband has been preceded by that of her half sister Helen to Menelaus; and in distant times by Althea, Scylla, and the Lemnian women.[2] The impending doom of Argos follows upon that of Troy. Repetition is emphasized in the very first words spoken, when the watchman says:

> I ask the gods some respite from the weariness
> of this watchtime measured by years I lie awake
> elbowed upon the Atreidae's roof dogwise to mark
> the grand processionals of all the stars of night.
>
> (*Ag.* 1-4)

And the one who waits upon the house is followed by those who wait within the city, the chorus of Argive elders who sing of the

[2] *Lib. Bear.* 594-638.

recent and the distant past. "Of old" much has occurred which is to be repeated in the peculiar circumstances of this drama. The ancient world of primitive myth stands behind the world of Troy and Argos which in turn stands between the Athens of Aeschylus' day and the fabled past. Hence the characters and events have a double reference throughout: to what has happened before the related action of the drama and to what has happened since in Athens as a modern Greek city.

Both the opening and the closing of the trilogy remind the audience that the past and present are struggling toward reconciliation. The closing scenes make the conflict between ancient and modern and the achievement of harmony evident, for the chorus of the Erinyes laments the fact that Athena and Apollo have overthrown an older order:

> Gods of the younger generation, you have ridden down
> the laws of the elder time, torn them out of my hands.
>
> (*Eum.* 778-779)

They accuse Athena of having cast out "the mind of the past."[3] Yet she reminds them that the future lies with Athens and the new order she, as the agent of Zeus, has established:

> Time
> in his forward flood shall ever grow more dignified
> for the people of this city.
>
> (*Eum.* 852-853)

Her prophecy of earthly prosperity for men who are well governed is confirmed by the reconciliation of past and present in the heavenly order as well as the earthly:

> There shall be peace forever between these people
> of Pallas and their guests. Zeus the all seeing
> met with Destiny to confirm it.
>
> (*Eum.* 1044-1046)

[3] H. D. F. Kitto sees the Erinyes as agents of the gods in bringing to justice the guilty Agamemnon and Clytemnestra. But it is important to emphasize the conflict between the Erinyes and the newer order of Zeus and Athena. The Erinyes are indeed agents of a wrathful Dike, but not thereby agents of Zeus. (*Form and Meaning in Drama* [London, 1956], pp. 30-31.)

Zeus and Destiny are reconciled just as, at Athena's persuasion, the people of Athens and the Eumenides are brought together. The significance of this conjunction and agreement of cosmic forces will become apparent later. To anticipate briefly, it is the condition for lawfulness in the city, and for harmony among men. The human abode can become secure only when the dissension of heaven is mitigated, only when Zeus has fought and won a battle in heaven that prefigures the battle on earth which ends in the ascendancy of Athens and its leadership among the Greek cities.

There has been, we are told, a succession of tyrannies among the gods, brought to an end at some distant time by Zeus:

> He who in time long ago was great,
> throbbing with gigantic strength,
> shall be as if he never were, unspoken.
> He who followed him has found
> his master, and is gone.
> Cry aloud without fear the victory of Zeus,
> you will not have failed the truth.
>
> (*Ag.* 167-175)

The first ruler was Uranus, overthrown by the second, Cronus, who in turn was vanquished by Zeus. In like manner among the earthly powers there has been conquest and defeat. Troy was defeated by the Greeks, some of them inhabitants of Argos, and in the present both Troy and Argos are to be ruled by the lawfulness and reason of Athens. Among both gods and men time brings changes: Zeus and the power of necessity or destiny are reconciled, just as the power of law and the rule of the city are finally brought to harmony.

The action of the *Oresteia* is at once cosmic, in the sense outlined above, and personal because the central figure, Orestes, is the human counterpart of the triumphant Zeus. The younger generation of gods have known in their own history what Orestes is to make known, through his suffering, to the human inhabitants of the *polis*. The suffering of Orestes is thus controlled and made meaningful by Zeus through his children Apollo and Athena. The intervention of the gods, then, is not capricious nor a dramatic "device," but rather an integral part of the total action. This is why the gods can be the teachers and leaders of men: there has been an evolution in heaven toward justice and right rule to serve as a pattern or "form" for a like history among men. But justice in the *polis* remains precarious, while in heaven it is with Zeus permanently fixed.

The parallel between Zeus and Orestes (brought out more clearly if the *Prometheus* and the *Oresteia* are compared), and the relationship between heavenly order and earthly order have been remarked by Friedrich Solmsen in his study of Aeschylus and Hesiod.[4]

We learn in the *Prometheus* that Zeus is endangered by the curse brought upon him by his overthrowing of Cronus. The Erinyes of his father menace him just as the Erinyes of Clytemnestra threaten Orestes. But both are saved, and the curse of Clytemnestra, like that of Cronus, becomes ineffective.[5] Solmsen draws the parallel in this manner:

> The stability of Zeus' reign, his escape from the legacy of the curse and crime to which he is heir, is predicated on the spirit in which he administers his reign. By changing his character and his policies Zeus paves the way to his reconciliation with Prometheus and the disclosure of the vital secret. It is justice and moderation which save him and ensure the eternal duration of his kindgom. Just as the Areopagus, the incorruptible organ of Justice will be forever a bulwark of Athens, so the spirit of justice will be the stabilizing factor for the world government of Zeus. In this new spirit of Justice, which once secured will not be lost, Zeus' rule has a guarantee of permanence which that of Uranus and Cronus lacked. Aeschylus accepts the tradition that Zeus came to his power by the use of violence; he even adds the motif that Zeus was threatened by his father's curse on that occasion. But this curse can be averted—as it can in the case of Orestes though not in that of Eteocles.[6]

When the specific events of the trilogy are thus placed in the larger framework of cosmic evolution the plot of the *Oresteia* in its literal manifestation may appear to diminish in dramatic in-

[4] *Hesiod and Aeschylus*, "Cornell Studies in Classical Philology," Vol. XXX (Ithaca, 1949).

[5] Cf. Solmsen, pp. 158-59, 161.

[6] *Hesiod and Aeschylus*, p. 163. Cf. E. T. Owen, *The Harmony of Aeschylus* (Toronto, 1952), p. 61. Also, G. Glotz, *La solidarité de la famille dans le droit criminel en Grèce* (Paris, 1904), pp. 408-13.

tensity, for the violent murders and invocations, the pursuit of Orestes by the Erinyes, the threats of the gods and the fearfulness of men become part of a larger design to be apprehended in those scenes and speeches which have appeared to some to be too abstract and theoretical. Yet to find the significance of the "duller" passages is precisely the way to an understanding of the trilogy as a whole.

If we see the work as a drama of murder and revenge it becomes melodramatic; the long introduction of the *Agamemnon* becomes burdensome, too dark and portentous for the killing of a king. Not only does the *Agamemnon* become too heavy for the following dramas, but the final trial scene fails to be meaningful. One commentator has well noted the first point, but has committed the very error he warns us of, for he cannot understand the significance of the trial. E. T. Owen has written:

> The *Agamemnon* by itself, judged as a single dramatic play of the Sophoclean type, cannot quite bear its own weight. The point, of course, is that it is not an independent piece; the "plot" of the *Agamemnon* is not Aeschylus' tragic plot, it is just the beginning of it; and the so-called prologue, besides being the imaginative and dramatic preparation for the action that follows within the play, is the grand overture to the whole trilogy. It puts before us the immense scene required for the action the poet designs, lifts our eyes to the horizons wide enough to contain it, and the drama of Agamemnon's death is, in that reference, as the first episode in the mighty drama of the *Oresteia*.[7]

And then he says of the trial scene, "but I suspect . . . that Aeschylus had his eye chiefly on the effectiveness of the projected trial scene, its effectiveness as a verbal quibbling match. He was preparing for those refinements and sophistries, the cleverness of which he thought would delight his audience." [8] We shall see later that this scene is no "verbal quibbling match," and that it too, like the "shades of fate whose shape we dimly see" has a portentousness beyond mere entertainment.

The significance of the past for the present action, and the bearing of the present upon the future is further elaborated by

---

[7] *The Harmony of Aeschylus*, pp. 81-82.
[8] *Ibid.*, p. 115.

relationships established between Orestes and other figures of a distant time. Just as Orestes' situation has certain elements in common with the former plight of Zeus, now the ruler of all creation, so too his position as a son is mirrored in the fate of heroes of old.

Superficially, Orestes' predicament is not an unusual one, for it is simply that of a son and heir sent into exile to prevent his succession to power. And his return, in the *Libation Bearers,* to avenge his father's death does not appear unusual until it is made known that he returned because Apollo commanded him to do so. Yet, what may appear at first to be an unusual involvement with the god and an even more uncommon conclusion is to a large extent anticipated in the fortunes of earlier sons, although the outcome of their suffering had not been as fortunate as Orestes' is to be. But the very point of the drama lies in this fact: that similar events have had far different outcomes previously, that what happens to Orestes marks a definite change in the conduct of both gods and men.

The earlier sons are alluded to in the drama and their fates compared to the present action. The first to offend was Ixion, referred to by Apollo as "the first murderer" when Apollo answers the charge that the Erinyes bring against the younger gods:

> CHORUS: You honor bloody actions where you have no right.
> The oracles you give shall be no longer clean.
> APOLLO: My father's purposes are twisted then. For he
> was appealed to by Ixion, the first murderer.[9]
>
> (*Eum.* 715-718)

The precedent for Apollo's defense of Orestes, the matricide, is to be found in Zeus' protection of Ixion, who murdered his father-in-law. After the act was committed Ixion, like Orestes, went mad. He was purified by Zeus (as Orestes is to be purified by Apollo) and admitted to Olympus. There he tried to seduce Hera and was cast into the nether world by Zeus, who devised the well-known punishment for him. Thus the new generation of gods, who are subordinate to Zeus, can claim that Zeus himself estab-

[9] Cf. *Eum.* 440-441: "a supplicant in the tradition of Ixion, sacrosanct."

lished a more lenient treatment for the crime of murder. But in the case of Ixion, as in the case of another offending son, Asclepius, there was a further transgression which brought terrible final punishment upon those two who were saved from immediate retribution.[10]

Indeed, there is an arresting relationship between Ixion and Asclepius that can be noted. On philological grounds it is highly speculative, for it rests upon the assumed fact that both names are derivations from the Greek for mistletoe (ἰξός). But on mythological grounds there is evidence that the two would be related in the minds of many Greeks for there is one version of the Ixion story which relates Ixion, Asclepius, and Apollo in a significant way.[11] In that account, Ixion is said to have had an adulterous relationship with Coronis when she was with child by Apollo. Some say Ixion was then killed by Zeus, others that he was killed by Apollo. But we need only note that the child which was saved was Asclepius, and recall his relationship to Apollo.

The circumstances surrounding the mythological heroes and

[10] The importance of Ixion is noted by Georges Méautis in his *Eschyle et la trilogie* (Paris, 1936), pp. 276-77. He states, "Ixion, c'est le myth de l'ingratitude humaine. Ayant tué son beau-père Eionée qui lui réclamait les présents de noce, Ixion s'enfuit à travers la terre repoussé de tous, car il était, comme Cain, le premier meurtrier, le premier homme qui eût versé le sang de sa propre famille. . . . Zeus, pris de pitié devant cette infinie détresse, reçut et purifia celui qui s'était constitué son suppliant. C'était bien là le 'don gratuit de la grace' et les traditions précisent bien que ce fut la pitié et la pitié seule qui fut le mobile de Zeus." * Although Meautis' emphasis upon "le don gratuit de la grace" interprets Zeus's action in terms too Christian, he is correct in noting the importance of this allusion in Apollo's argument. Pindar (*Second Pythian Ode,* 32) refers to Ixion as the first to shed the blood of kindred with willful intent.

* "Ixion is the myth of human ingratitude. Having killed his father-in-law Eioneus who demanded the wedding presents, Ixion fled across the earth, driven away by everyone because he was, like Cain, the first murderer, the first man who had shed the blood of his own family. . . . Zeus, seized with pity before such great suffering, received and purified him who had become his suppliant. That was indeed the 'gratuitous gift of grace,' and the traditions specify that it was pity and only pity which moved Zeus."

[11] On the derivation of the names, cf. Rendel Harris, *The Ascent of Olympus* (Manchester, 1917), Ch. II. Also, Robert Graves, *The Greek Myths* (Baltimore, 1955), Vol. II.

Apollo are similar to Orestes' involvement with the god. All three are related to Apollo in terms of a problem that has to do with the significance of the marriage bond.

Apollo, so the story goes, fell in love with Coronis, daughter of Phlegyas. When she was with child by the god she transgressed the marriage covenant by, as one version has it, arranging a marriage with a mortal; or, as the other version states, committing adultery with Ixion. At Apollo's request Coronis was killed by Artemis and the living child taken (some versions say cut from the womb by Hermes) to the safe keeping of Chiron from whom Asclepius learned the sacred art of healing.[12]

Asclepius, after learning the art of healing from Chiron, offended the gods by using his skill to bestow immortal life upon man. There are two references to Asclepius' *hubris* in the *Oresteia* and both are coupled with the distinction between the immortal gods and mortal man:

> CHORUS: But when the black and mortal blood of man
> has fallen to the ground before his feet, who then
> can sing spells to call it back again?
> Did Zeus not warn us once
> when he struck to impotence
> that one who could in truth charm back the dead men?
> Had the gods not so ordained
> that fate should stand against fate
> to check any man's excess,
> my heart now would have outrun speech
> to break forth the water of its grief.
>
> (*Ag.* 1019-1029)

The gods, at least among themselves, are not accountable for their actions as men are:

> APOLLO: Zeus could undo shackles, such hurt can be made good,
> and there is every kind of way to get out. But once

[12] Note that Apollo took revenge on Coronis for breaking the marriage covenant just as he did later on Cassandra for the same offense. Both within the drama, then, and in the mythological past behind the action Apollo is one who has been cheated and misled by women, and who, quite naturally, stands for the rights of the male.

the dust has drained down all a man's blood, once the
   man
has died, there is no raising of him up again.
This is a thing for which my father never made
curative spells. All other states, without effort
of hard breath, he can completely rearrange.

(Eum. 645-651)

Thus Apollo answers the Erinyes when they point out that
Zeus is guilty of overthrowing his father, and consequently ought
not to object to Agamemnon's death by his wife's hand. But the
difference between mortal and immortal is radical: among the
gods the hurt of violence can be made good, while among men a
violent act once committed is irrevocable. Even the gods are pow-
erless to restore the dead to life; this is the one thing for which
there are no "curative spells." Yet Asclepius used his medical art
to bring the dead to life, and for that he was struck "with a lurid
thunderbolt and killed" by Zeus, who, in taking revenge, is seeing
to it that the unalterable order of things is preserved.

Yet Asclepius became, after death, an immortal being, like
Herakles. He remains the patron hero of the healing art. Orestes
too, we know, was venerated as a hero, for he was elevated to the
position of a demigod the nature of whom we will inquire into
later.

There is yet a further relationship between Orestes and Asclepius that needs to be touched upon, but with the greatest care.
It has been noted that the image of the dog and the snake occur
throughout the *Oresteia,* particularly in conjunction with Clytemnestra and the avenging Erinyes. Clytemnestra is referred to
as a dog, a bitch; she dreams of suckling a snake; and her Erinyes
are called "dog-like" and appear to Orestes, in his madness, as
snakes.[13] In relation to the Erinyes the dog and the snake are
creatures of guilt and vengeance. But in relation to Asclepius
they were the instruments of his curative powers. The dog that
accompanied him was enabled to cure wounds and ulcers by lick-

[13] For a full discussion of these images, see Philip Wheelwright, *The Burning Fountain* (Bloomington, Indiana, 1954), Ch. XII. Other references to the
Erinyes as hounds of vengeance, *Lib. Bear.* 1053-1054, 1057-1058; as snakes or
part snake, *Lib. Bear.* 527, 928, 1048-1050, *Eum.* 46-53, 184.

ing them; the snake to cure injured parts of the body and impregnate sterile women.[14] Thus the dog and the snake have a double meaning in the *Oresteia:* in the reign of the early, chthonian gods (the Erinyes) they are agents of vengeance; while in the reign of the new gods, in which Asclepius appears, they are curative and purifying. The dog and the snake which formerly hunted men down and drove them mad can become healing agents, just as Apollo, Asclepius, and the new order of gods under Zeus become the instruments for justice. Orestes then must make his peace with the dog-like, snake-like Erinyes. He does so through the divine aid of Apollo and Athena, one the healer-god, the other the god who can persuade the Erinyes to give up their former role and become guardians of the welfare of the city.[15]

Orestes, the dramatic hero, is the counterpart of the earlier hero who was saved by Apollo. As with Asclepius, Apollo wishes to give Orestes vital knowledge. But the power and wisdom bestowed upon Orestes is neither the freedom of licentiousness given to Ixion, nor the magical healing art given to Asclepius, but rather the grace of purgation, freedom from pollution and madness, and the knowledge of a justice above and more powerful than the blood morality of his own house and city. He makes clear what he has received:

> I have been beaten and been taught, I understand
> the many rules of absolution, where it is right
> to speak and where be silent. In this action now
> speech has been ordered by my teacher, who is wise.
> The stain of blood dulls now and fades upon my hand.
> My blot of matricide is being washed away.
>
> (*Eum.* 276-281)

The plot of the *Oresteia* is the action of Orestes as he comes to this new knowledge and purification. In both the dramatic and

[14] For a discussion of the Asclepius cult, see Lewis Richard Farnell, *Greek Hero Cults and Ideas of Immortality* (Oxford, 1921), Ch. X. Also, E. J. and L. Edelstein, *Asclepius: A Collection and Interpretation of the Testimonies* (Baltimore, 1945).

[15] For a discussion of the form of the Erinyes, see Jane Harrison, *Themis, A Study of the Social Origins of Greek Religion* (2nd ed. revised; Cambridge, England, 1927), Chs. VIII, IX. Also her *Prolegomena to the Study of Greek Religion* (3rd ed.; Cambridge, England, 1922), Ch. V.

the ritualistic sense then he is a hero, like the hero Asclepius whom he in some ways resembles.

In the conventional dramatic sense Orestes is the "hero" of the *Oresteia;* but to a Greek audience he would have been a hero in the cult sense too, for he was worshiped in some localities as saints are worshiped today. Thus Aeschylus is working not only with myths, not only with stories of a dim past which might or might not be accepted as historically accurate by the Athenians, but also with mythological figures whose status in the present would be of heroes, that is, venerated semi-divine intermediaries between gods and men whose heroic stature is explained in the drama.[16]

The suffering and eventual acquittal of Orestes explains his mortal life which endows him with the prerequisites for the heroic role later conferred upon him. Yet Orestes is a hero whose relationship to the Olympian gods is different from that of the heroes of a more ancient time. The action of Orestes within the drama is intended to exhibit that relationship, for the gods with whom Orestes is allied, the Olympian immortals who save and sanctify him, are different from the gods with whom the other hero, Agamemnon, is related. Or rather, it should be said that the older generation of Agamemnon and Clytemnestra maintain a more primitive and less understanding relationship with the new Olympian gods, partly due to the fact that they still maintain a relationship with the older order of gods represented by the chthonian forces, especially the Erinyes. In short, just as the older and newer generations of gods are in conflict, so the older and newer generations of heroes are in conflict. The *Oresteia* has as one of its dramatic themes the development of a new kind of hero and hero worship out of a more primitive hero worship which is revealed in the first two plays of the trilogy.

There is, of course, a social and religious tradition behind this dramatic treatment of the hero and his relationship to the Olympian gods. Just what the religious beliefs and practices were it is difficult to say with assurance, but it is likely that there were two

[16] The religious significance of heroes is discussed by Jane Harrison, *Themis,* Ch. VIII.

strands of religious belief, one of more ancient origin perhaps than the other, in the Athens of Aeschylus' day. Fustel de Coulanges has drawn the distinction in a manner that accords well with the dramatic action of the *Oresteia:*

> Thus in this race [the Greeks] the religious idea presented itself under two different forms. On the one hand, man attached the divine attribute to the invisible principles, to the intelligence, to what he perceived of the soul, to what of the sacred he felt in himself. On the other hand, he applied his ideas of the divine to the external object which he saw, which he loved or feared; to physical agents that were the masters of his happiness and of his life.
>
> These two orders of belief laid the foundation of two religions that lasted as long as Greek and Roman society. They did not make war upon each other; they even lived on very good terms, and shared the empire over man; but they never became confounded. Their dogmas were always entirely distinct, often contradictory; and their ceremonies and practices were absolutely different. The worship of the gods of Olympus and that of heroes and manes never had anything common between them. Which of these two religions was the earlier in date no one can tell. It is certain, however, that one—that of the dead—having been fixed at a very early epoch, always remained unchangeable in its practices, while its dogmas faded away little by little; the other—that of physical nature—was more progressive, and developed freely from age to age, modifying its legends and doctrines by degrees, and continually augmenting its authority over men.[17]

For the family as well as for a group of citizens united in the *polis,* the hero, whether ancestor or local hieratic hero-god, came to be the spokesman and representative of the individual man to the divine Olympian deities. Orestes, at the conclusion of the drama, is enabled through the intervention of Apollo and Athena to take his place as such a type. From this point of view the *Oresteia* is the dramatic presentation of how Orestes became a hero,[18] endowed with the potency of intermediary and protector.

[17] *The Ancient City* (12th ed.; Boston, 1901; reprinted, New York, 1955), pp. 121-22.

[18] Bruno Snell points out that the action in the *Eumenides* is not concerned with the decision of a man taking action, but rather with the fate of a man, what his destiny is to be. "Sonderbarerweise ist dies nicht die Entscheidung eines handelnden Menschen, sondern die Entscheidung über einen

This semi-divine role, once attributed to the dead ancestors about whose tombs family worship centered, is gradually transferred to cultural heroes. Georges Méautis has characterized them as follows:

> Les héros sont des êtres protecteurs, incarnation même de l'idée de patrie. Ils sont donc les gardiens de l'ordre établi, ils ont leur place, à côté des dieux, dans les formules de serment.[19]

That Orestes will become the protector, guardian, and teacher of his people in Argos is made clear by his plea to Athena that she save him, his promise of loyalty to her as the consequence, and his assertion that he will return home as an enlightened ruler who shall be a power among his people even from the grave:

> Now it is from pure mouth and with good auspices
> I call upon Athene, queen of this land, to come
> and rescue me. She, without work of her spear, shall win
> myself and all my land and all the Argive host
> to stand her staunch companion for the rest of time.
>
> (*Eum.* 287-291)

> Pallas Athene, you have kept my house alive.
> When I had lost the land of my fathers you gave me
> a place to live. Among the Hellenes they shall say:
> "A man of Argos lives again in the estates
> of his father, all by grace of Pallas Athene, and
> Apollo, and with them the all-ordaining god
> the Savior"—who remembers my father's death, who looked
> upon my mother's advocates, and rescues me.
> I shall go home now, but before I go I swear
> to this your country and to this your multitude
> of people into all the bigness of time to be,
> that never man who holds the helm of my state shall come

Menschen, die Abstimmung über das Schicksal des Orest" * ("Aischylos und das Handeln im Drama," *Philologus*, Supplement Band XX, Heft 1 [Leipzig, 1928]). Jacoby asserts that "a connection between him [Orestes] and the Areopagus does not exist before Aischylos" (*Atthis* [Oxford, 1949], p. 263, note 156).

* "Strangely enough, this is not the decision of an acting man, but the decision over a man: the jury's verdict over the fate of Orestes."

[19] "The heroes are protective beings, the very incarnation of the idea of the native country. They are therefore the guardians of the established order; they have their place beside the gods in the formula of the oath" ("L'Oedipe à Colone et le cult des héros," *Recueil de travaux publiés par la faculté des lettres*, No. 19 [Neuchâtel, 1940], p. 19).

against your country in the ordered strength of spears,
but though I lie then in my grave, I still shall wreak
helpless bad luck and misadventure upon all
who stride across the oath that I have sworn.

(Eum. 754-769)

This dramatic outcome allows us to say that the action of the
Oresteia is, in respect to the hero, Orestes, the representation of
what a hero truly is. The condition for his elevation to the position of hero is an allegiance to the younger generation of gods in
recognition of their moral superiority.

But this is not the traditional origin of heroes. Formerly, heroes
and gods were clearly distinguished both in origin and power;
now, with the benevolent hero regarded as a semi-divine leader
of the *polis* (somewhat like Plato's conception of the Divine
Shepherd who stands above the statesman in the wisdom of kingship and rule, and who could rule without laws because he knows
the ways of the gods and what is right) [20] the hero becomes one
who has been taught and purified by the Olympian deities.

Traditionally, the hero was identified with the chthonian powers, inhabitants of a subterranean spiritual realm that was opposed to the heavenly realm of the Olympian gods. The following
description of Georges Méautis makes clear what their position
was:

Les héros sont, donc, avant tout, des divinités *chthoniennes,* issues
de la terre; leur symbole est fréquement le serpent, cet être mystéri-
eux qui sort brusquement du sol et y rentre à nouveau. . . . Bien,
plus encore, alors que les sacrifices aux dieux étaient célébrés de
jour, les sacrifices aux héros, comme ceux des Erinyes, s'offraient de
nuit. Il y avait donc, chez les héros, quelque chose de sombre,
d'inquiétant, qui les séparait nettement des dieux lumineux de
l'Olympe. Loin de servir d'intermédiaires entre la terre et le ciel,
ils appartiennent à un mode special, fait de colères, de rancunes.
Leur puissance est plus souvent malfaisante que bienfaisante. Il
convient bien davantage de les apaiser que l'implorer leurs faveurs.[21]

[20] *Statesman* 294. Also, see *Laws* IV, 713ff.; IX, 853c. Plato tells the story of
the earliest legislators, daimons, who furnished peace, justice, and order to
mankind. Unlike Aeschylus, he places this time in the reign of Cronus.

[21] "The heroes were therefore, before all else, chthonian divinities, born of
the earth; their symbol is often the serpent, that mysterious being who appears unexpectedly from the soil and disappears into it again. . . . Moreover,

This attitude of respect, terror, and veneration was attached to the tomb of the hero where offerings were made to his shade and his help implored in the hope that his vengeful spirit would be placated. The great scene at the tomb of Agamemnon in the *Libation Bearers* (306-509) is an excellent illustration of the relationship in which the suppliant stood to the power of the hero.

But the young man Orestes is, in comparison with his father, a new kind of hero: one who, like the younger gods, is concerned not with blood vengeance and the protection of the family, but with the benevolent guidance of men living together in the city. In the dramatic presentations of both Aeschylus and Sophocles the hero as semi-divine shepherd of the people comes to take the place of the hero as ancestral spirit of familial justice. Oedipus, as he appears in the Colonus play, is endowed with the magical powers of divinity as well as the wisdom to guarantee right rule and peace to the city of Athens. In the *Oresteia* there is a representation of how the hero has changed from a fearful spirit of vengeance whose main concern is to see that the morality of blood is enforced, to one who is endowed with divine power for the good of the *polis*.[22] The nature of gods and heroes is truly one of the central themes of the *Oresteia,* and it is exhibited through the hero of the drama, Orestes, as his action unfolds.

The dramatic statement that Orestes is a new kind of hero whose power works for justice in the community is part of the resolution effected by the *Oresteia.* The conflict between the old and the new order of the gods requires a resolution not only between Zeus and Destiny but also between men and the immor-

---

while the sacrifices to the gods were celebrated in the daytime, the sacrifices to the heroes, like those of the Erinyes, were made at night. Accordingly, there was something somber about the heroes, something disquieting, which sharply distinguished them from the luminous gods of Olympus. Far from serving as intermediaries between earth and heaven, they belonged to a peculiar class, made of wrath and spite. Their power is more often malicious than kind. It is much more suitable to appease them than to ask their good will" ("L'Oedipe à Colone," p. 10).

[22] A discussion of this change is to be found in Victor Ehrenberg, *The Greek State* (New York, 1960), sec. I.3. See also Friedrich Solmsen, "Strata of Greek Religion in Aeschylus," *Harvard Theological Review,* XL (1940), 211-26.

tals. While the old order insisted that the dead haunt the living, the new order proclaims that the ancestor instructs, guides, and manifests himself as a beneficent force in the *polis*. This new outlook is responsible for a general clarification of religious attitudes and practices. It is presupposed by the new social order established by Athena, for justice cannot be realized if the ancestor-heroes are malignant since they then enforce observances, actions, and sentiments of fear beyond the control of the human rulers of the community. It is also required by the new conception of the cosmos, for the traditional supernatural beings must have their dominions and powers defined.

Aeschylus establishes the hero as a man who understands what it is most important for men to know, the ancient powers of blood morality as guardians of the city's well-being. While the old religious order declared the dead must be placated because they are revengeful, and venerated because they can bestow fertility, the new religious order gives to the old gods, the Erinyes, the power of assuring fertility, and to the new heroes the knowledge of right rule and civic harmony.

The hero Orestes receives his instruction not in his own land but in the city of Athens. Orestes is no longer the local hero-god of ancestral origin; he connects his cult and his veneration with a wider religious world. The new hero brings the parochial cult into direct relation with the universal Olympian gods. The *Oresteia* not only exhibits this change but encourages it as contributing to political health. The old religious order, because it placed the clan and cult heroes at the center of worship, tended to perpetuate the smaller political units among which there would be, inevitably, considerable conflict. The new religious order does not deny the importance of the local hero, in this case Orestes, but forces him into the cosmic order established by the new gods.

This clarification of heroic role under the order of Zeus is part of a developing moral vision that the next chapter will consider.

CHAPTER THREE

THE MORAL ISSUE:
GODS AND MEN; MALE AND FEMALE

Three cosmologically and historically determined stages of development have been discovered in the *Oresteia*. The world of Olympian revolution is midway between the established order of the older gods and the enlightened *politeia* of Athens. Orestes finds himself caught up in the conflict between representatives of an old and a new cosmic order which is resolved in fifth-century Athens. Dramatically the presentation makes all actors contemporaries; but mythologically and historically they are separated in time. Aeschylus has not used myth simply as the subject of his drama, but has placed myth in a setting of contemporary political institutions. Thus the Athens of Aeschylus' day is able to participate in and, as it were, redirect the events of the past.

The *Oresteia* is a self-conscious historical drama embracing what ordinarily lies outside of history. This integration of the mythological and the historical is what gives the *Oresteia* its peculiar dramatic power, for this technique reinforces the moral theme which lies at the center of the action. Orestes exists outside the ordinary course of political events, yet is made to participate in political events. Myth is endowed with the cares of communal life, and the human city reaffirms its dependence upon a cosmic order reflected in myth. In this way Aeschylus achieves a double perspective: he leads us to regard what ordinarily is taken to be immutable, existing out of time, as suffering the development of the temporal; and to recognize in the history of cities a reflection of the permanent order of the cosmos. The celestial and the terrestrial participate each in the order of the other.

In this respect Aeschylus is not Platonistic in his conception of the cosmos, the *polis,* and their relationship. Perhaps it is for this reason that Plato criticizes Aeschylus, since Aeschylus endows the paradigmatic reality with a principle of becoming, and bestows upon the order of appearance a political excellence Plato was by experience and ontological commitment unable to accept.[1]

Aeschylus establishes his view of the change first through the Erinyes' insistence that justice is realized through the repetition of permanently fixed patterns, and then through the demonstration that the younger gods under Zeus have broken the pattern in the cosmos and singled out Orestes to break the pattern in the human realm. Orestes, in being forced out of the house into the city, is at the same time forced out of his role as mythic hero into the role of historical character. Hence it is through him that the modern city is related to its primitive forerunners.

According to the ancient story, which may, it is conjectured, go back far beyond Mycenaean times, Orestes and his sisters, Iphigenia and Electra, have suffered for the crimes of their ancestors.[2] The fate of each of the children moves toward the restoration of the House of Atreus through the son. It is appropriate that his destiny should bring the chain of crimes to its end, for the son of the house is the one through whom the name and worship of the house are perpetuated. Upon the death of the father the son assumes the role of priest and family leader, a responsibility that cannot be assumed by the wife or daughter. Hence Orestes' absence at Agamemnon's return, and his obligation after the death of the king are of the greatest significance.[3]

The continuation of the ruling house, and hence the survival of Argos, are at stake. Clytemnestra dares to assume that through her as absolute ruler, not as regent, the house and city can be preserved. To this end she had Orestes sent away, but his exile could never be the means of frustrating what has been divinely com-

[1] Plato's criticism of the dramatists is ably discussed by Paul Vicaire, *Platon, critique littéraire* (Paris, 1960), especially I, 2, Ch. V.

[2] T. B. L. Webster points out that the names "Agamemnon," "Thyestes," "Orestes" are found on the Pylos tablets. (*From Mycenae to Homer* [London, 1958], p. 121.)

[3] "Thus the father," Coulanges has written, "is convinced that his destiny after this life will depend upon the care his son will take of his tomb, and the son, on his part, is convinced that his father will become a god after death, whom he will have to invoke" (*The Ancient City*, p. 98). A discussion of Coulanges' views on descent will be found in Nares Chandra Sen-Gupta, *The Evolution of Law* (2nd ed.; Calcutta, 1951), Ch. XII.

manded. Orestes survives to return and exact vengeance. And his exile has a special relevance for the greater moral issue that the drama considers. Through his wanderings which brought him to other peoples and other forms of worship, Orestes has come to question the ancestral morality that has controlled the actions and judgments of the ruling Argive family.

This explains why Orestes is in outlook so obviously different from the remaining members of the family. It appears that his exile has prepared him for the role of the mortal through whom the moral enlightenment is to take place. When he first returns he stands between the claims of two different moralities, each precise and exacting, each represented by a generation of divinities. He is a member of a family which has been ruled by the ancestral morality upheld by the Erinyes, a morality that assumes a set of values and obligations. Yet he is ordered to return and seek vengeance by a god, Apollo, who is to be instrumental in establishing within the *polis* a morality that rests upon a different set of values and obligations.

It would be a mistake to see the two moralities as contradictory; they are not. Both Apollo and Athena agree with the Erinyes on a number of issues, as we will see. But initially, with the confrontation of Orestes and Electra in the second drama, the contrary demands of the two moralities are emphasized.[4]

The terrifying trial that Orestes and Electra face is evident from the atmosphere of gloom and wanhope in which the *Libation Bearers* opens. If the guile and violence of the older generation are not overcome the hope of just action is doomed. The children of the house, as Electra says, are the hope of the house. From the image used in her speech it is clear that they are to be instrumental in even a greater achievement:

> Hear one more cry, father, from me. It is my last.
> Your nestlings huddle suppliant at your tomb: look forth
> and pity them, female with the male strain alike.
> Do not wipe out this seed of the Pelopidae.
> So, though you died, you shall not yet be dead, for when

[4] For a comparison of the two moralities, see Solmsen, *Hesiod and Aeschylus*, p. 187.

a man dies, children are the voice of his salvation
afterward. Like corks upon the net, these hold
the drenched and flaxen meshes, and they will not drown.[5]

(Lib. Bear. 500-507)

The net they sustain is at once the net of treachery and the net of
fate. In getting revenge they are the agents of destiny. The stir-
ring chant of Orestes confirms this:

Ἄρης Ἄρει ξυμβαλεῖ, Δίκᾳ Δίκα.

("Warstrength shall collide with warstrength; right with right.")

(Lib. Bear. 461)

The two surviving children have got to muster the strength for
the overthrow of the usurpers; with them is the memory of the
sister sacrificed:

The secret anger remembers the child that shall be avenged.

(Ag. 155)

Each of the children carries the cosmic evolution further along its
course: first Iphigenia in her innocence, sacrificed for an evil
cause, then Electra in her single-mindedness of revenge, and
finally Orestes in his act of matricide. The role thrust upon each
child is meaningful in this larger action. The passivity and suffering of Iphigenia, treated as a beast of sacrifice (note Aeschylus'
use of λέπαδνον, yoke strap, and χαλινῶν, bridle bit, in the description of the sacrifice) contrasts sharply with the vengeful Electra
who is afraid of falling into her mother's excesses:

And for myself, grant that I be more temperate
of heart than my mother; that I act with purer hand.

(Lib. Bear. 140-141)

Orestes, though he willingly takes on the task of revenge, stands
in a different relationship to their parents from Electra. She is
close to Clytemnestra for she shares the passionate intensity of

---

[5] The text is difficult here. It is not clear whether these words are spoken
by Electra or Orestes. Verrall excludes them on the ground that Clement
attributes them to Sophocles. But the imagery and thought are so consistent
and appropriate that there is little doubt of their genuineness.

women, and like her mother is ready to use the darker powers of
the *chthonioi:*

> May Zeus, from all shoulder's strength,
> pound down his fist upon them,
> ohay, smash their heads.
> Let the land once more believe.
> There has been wrong done. I ask for right.
> Hear me, Earth. Hear me, grandeurs of Darkness.
>
> (*Lib. Bear.* 394-399)

Orestes, although bent on revenge, makes known his confusion
and fear:

> Hear me, you lordships of the world below.
> Behold in assembled power, curses from the dead,
> behold the last of the sons of Atreus, foundering
> lost, without future, cast
> from house and right. O god, where shall we turn? [6]
>
> (*Lib. Bear.* 405-409)

The *kommos* turns on the assumption of the very morality which
is to be questioned and finally modified. Orestes participates in a
ritualistic invocation of the dead even though he himself cannot
unquestioningly accept that blood for blood is the fitting moral
rule; but he is strengthened in what he accepts as his duty, for the
kommos ends with his determination to kill Clytemnestra (cf.
lines 438, 461). The chorus states the principle at the opening of
the *kommos* and concludes with the determination Orestes must
display:

> For the word of hatred spoken, let hate
> be a word fulfilled. The spirit of Right
> cries out aloud and exacts atonement
> due: blood stroke for the stroke of blood
> shall be paid. Who acts, shall endure. So speaks
> the voice of the age-old wisdom.
>
> The rest is action. Since your heart is set
> that way, now you must strike and prove your destiny.
>
> (*Lib. Bear.* 309-314; 512-513)

---

[6] A good discussion of the *kommos* in the *Libation Bearers* is to be found
in E. T. Owen, *The Harmony of Aeschylus,* pp. 93ff.

But at the final moment, when Orestes is about to kill Clytemnestra, he hesitates and asks advice of his companion, Pylades:

> ORESTES: What shall I do, Pylades? Be shamed to kill my mother?
> PYLADES: What then becomes thereafter of the oracles
> declared by Loxias at Pytho? What of sworn oaths?
> Count all men hateful to you rather than the gods.
>   (*Lib. Bear.* 899-903)

While Pylades is the voice of Apollonian conscience speaking within Orestes, ultimately Orestes himself comes to understand the meaning of the words spoken. Initially he is confused and guilty over what he is forced to do; lacking the directness of Electra, he needs to bring himself to the pitch of anger sufficient for revenge. To do this he considers all the reasons he has to kill Clytemnestra, and adds to those the punishments Apollo has threatened should he fail. But the fact is he never can bring himself to the point of believing he *ought* to do it; he attains the courage to do it not through moral obligations and duty, but through fear of consequences. His perplexity is intense:

> Shall I not trust such oracles as this? Or if
> I do not trust them, here is work that must be done.
> Here numerous desires converge to drive me on:
> the god's urgency and my father's passion, and
> with these the loss of my estates wears hard on me.
>   (*Lib. Bear.* 297-301)

All these are facts which might strengthen his resolve, but they are reasons which he needs to hold consciously before his mind. Orestes does not feel within himself the conviction that the act ought to be committed; he must do what he is loath to do because a powerful god whom he honors has commanded it.

Thus Orestes stands in contrast to those characters whose actions have been proof of their conviction that violent reprisal for bloodshed is right. In him conscience enjoins forbearance, reflection, restraint. In Clytemnestra, and in Agamemnon, who desecrated the altars of Troy, deep savage passions have dictated action. This kind of behavior is associated with the demonic forces of the underworld; and Orestes has been counseled to his matricide by a god of heaven. Thus a grave difficulty presents itself to him: how can a god who supports a rational morality demand blood for blood? Orestes cannot know that he is directed to act on behalf of a further purpose; he does not know that the crime is committed in order that it may be judged. It is this moral dilemma which drives him mad. He is caught between the demands of his family, his obligation to his father and his mother, to his household gods and the Erinyes of his murdered father, and the commandment of the gods of Olympus.[7]

As the sole surviving male member of the house of Atreus Orestes must contend with those who have usurped the power and right which should descend to him. His mother, Clytemnestra, has taken what is, according to ancestral morality, his own; yet to regain his lands and power he must commit matricide. His reluctance to do that stems not only from his horror of the crime as such, but also from the difficulty of the task.

Clytemnestra is no ordinary woman; she is formidable both personally and dramatically: she is not to be lightly dispatched.[8] Her dramatic stature is evident, first of all, from the fact that she appears significantly in all three of the plays, the only character to do so. Further, she has been the ruler of Argos: a woman taking upon herself the role of a man (she is described as possessing

[7] In arguing that Orestes faces a serious moral problem I relate the action of the *Libation Bearers* to the trial scene of the *Eumenides*. The moral resolution is in part exhibited through character. Orestes does change in the course of the action; the drama makes the change explicit even though the technique employed is not that of our own time. In this I differ with H. D. F. Kitto who argues that "Orestes is not this kind of tragic hero, that his character and his inner conflict are only a small part of the real drama" (*Form and Meaning in Drama* [London, 1956], p. 40). If by character and inner conflict we mean something of the sort that distinguishes Hamlet, then Orestes is not that sort of hero; but if by conflict we include, as I do, the antagonism between ways of explaining and justifying human action morally, then Orestes is a character who carries a conflict within himself. Here inner conflicts are reflections and exemplifications of outer conflicts.

[8] See the excellent article by R. P. Winnington-Ingram, "Clytemnestra and the Vote of Athena," *The Journal of Hellenic Studies*, LXVIII (1948), 130-47. The argument here is confirmed by his interpretation which emphasizes the importance of the marriage relationship and Clytemnestra's masculinity.

"male strength of heart in its high confidence"). She promises Aegisthus, at the conclusion of the first play that

> . . . you and I
> have the power; we two shall bring good order
> to our house at least.
>
> (*Ag.* 1672-3)

She desires order in the city, she wishes to placate the elders of Argos (*Ag.* 1654-1661), she wishes to rule well. But it is fated otherwise, and she is not capable of statesmanship, both because she is a mortal woman and because she is an ally of powerful forces in the chthonian world. She communicates with the Erinyes as a priestess of black magic:

> Yet I have given you much to lap up, outpourings
> without wine, sober propitiations, sacrificed
> in secrecy of night and on a hearth of fire
> for you, at an hour given to no other god.
>
> (*Eum.* 106-109)

The control she does gain over Argos is achieved through treachery, adultery, and terror. She has destroyed the foundations of the family, yet it is through the ancestral moral order that she would rule.[9] She has woven a net of treachery, her own part of that design often referred to in the play as the net of fate and death, and with this as her mantle of authority has taken control of the city.[10]

Clytemnestra is to be overcome finally by another woman, likewise one who rules, but one who rules by divine authority of Zeus: Athena. She too is a weaver, but one who, like Plato's Statesman, weaves a design of justice and right rule. It is a far different design from that Clytemnestra would compose. Into the cloth of character, friendship, and harmonious city life are woven many strands. Athena commands all the arts which Plato tells us the statesman must possess: oratory, generalship, and judging. That

[9] Adultery was the greatest offense to the family gods. Cf. Coulanges, *The Ancient City*, Ch. IX.

[10] The net imagery appears throughout: *Ag.* 866-868, 1047-1049, 1116-1117, 1381-1383, 1492-1493, 1610-1611; *Lib. Bear.* 248, 506-507, 997-1004; *Eum.* 110-113, 633-635.

Athena excels in oratory is evidenced by her successful persuasion of the Erinyes to become peaceful guardians of the hearth, Eumenides. Her excellence in generalship is proved by her direction of the armies of the Greek hosts (she is taking over Troy when called to the trial of Orestes); in judging it is demonstrated by her submission of the final decision in Orestes' trial.[11] In each of these respects Clytemnestra is deficient, and her effort to rule Argos is thus doomed to frustration.[12]

Her designs are destined to fail for another reason: she is a woman, and unlike Athena who is born of Zeus and has no mother, subject to the passions of her sex. Throughout the trilogy the dangers of female passion are emphasized. Not only does Cassandra warn of it:

> See there, see there! Keep from his mate the bull.
> Caught in the folded web's
> entanglement she pinions him and with the black horn
> strikes. And he crumples in the watered bath.
> Guile, I tell you, and death there in the caldron wrought.
>
> (*Ag.* 1125-1129)

But also the chorus of foreign serving-women in the *Libation Bearers* sings of the danger of impassioned women:

> But who can recount all
> the high daring in the will
> of man, and in the stubborn hearts of women
> the all-adventurous passions
> that couple with man's overthrow.

[11] "There is an art which controls all these arts. It is concerned with the laws and with all that belongs in the life of the community. It weaves all into its unified fabric with perfect skill. It is a universal art and so we call it by a name of universal scope. That name is one which I believe to belong to this art and to this alone, the name of Statesmanship" (Plato *Statesman* 305e ff., tr. J. B. Skemp).

[12] Winnington-Ingram ("Clytemnestra and the Vote of Athena," pp. 144-46) points out that Aeschylus regards the problem of woman's place in society as unsolved. "This tragedy, given its final touch of irony by the words of Athena, is absolute, since it was impossible in Clytemnestra's own society, and equally impossible in democratic Athens, for a woman of dominating will and intelligence to exploit her gifts to her own satisfaction and for the advantage of the community."

> The female force, the desperate
> love crams its resisted way
> on marriage and the dark embrace
> of brute beasts, of mortal men.
>
> (*Lib. Bear.* 594-602)

Clytemnestra's dangerously passionate nature is clearly drawn in her exultation after the murder of Agamemnon:

> Thus have I wrought, and I will not deny it now.
> That he might not escape nor beat aside his death,
> as fishermen cast their huge circling nets, I spread
> deadly abundance of rich robes, and caught him fast.
> I struck him twice. In two great cries of agony
> he buckled at the knees and fell. When he was down
> I struck him the third blow, in thanks and reverence
> to Zeus the lord of dead men underneath the ground.
> Thus he went down, and the life struggled out of him;
> and as he died he spattered me with the dark red
> and violent driven rain of bitter savored blood
> to make me glad, as gardens stand among the showers
> of God in glory at the birthtime of the buds.
>
> (*Ag.* 1380-1392)

Like her half sister Helen, she is the personification of Até and treachery.

It is made clear that both women have brought destruction to their families and to any who have opposed them when Cassandra says of Clytemnestra:

> This is the woman-lioness, who goes to bed
> with the wolf, when her proud lion ranges far away,
> and she will cut me down,
>
> (*Ag.* 1258-1260)

and when the chorus says of Helen:

> She left among her people the stir and clamor
> of shields and of spearheads,
> the ships to sail and the armor.
> She took to Ilium her dowry, death.
> She stepped forth lightly between the gates
> daring beyond all daring. And the prophets
> about the great house wept aloud and spoke:

"Alas, alas for the house and for the champions,
alas for the bed signed with their love together."

(*Ag.* 404-411)

The character of Helen emerges clearly through the comparisons between her and her sister that are implied throughout. The role she plays in the drama has been well stated by Méautis:

Un être est en execration à toute la Grèce, Hélène, pour qui se sont tués tant de héros sous les murs de Troie, c'est elle que chacun voudrait voir périr, juste vengeance de tant de malheurs semé sous ses pas. Mais les dieux en ont jugé autrement, ils sauvent cette femme abhorrée. Pour Eschyle, Hélène, était le symbole du désir, l'équivalent grec de l'orientale Maia.[13]

Helen seduced the whole of Troy and brought destruction upon the city; Clytemnestra seduced her lord and king (cf. *Ag.* 914-949) and brought ruin upon Argos. If they had been ruled by their husbands this needless death would have been prevented (*Ag.* 427-449).

Orestes has to contend with women, and he does not share their deadly frenzy. None of the men do; there is a distinct difference between male and female temperament clearly set forth in the characters of the drama. Recognition of this innate difference is a necessary condition for the establishment of right rule. Ancestral morality, which misunderstands this difference, can never realize the condition for the achievement of proper order between men and women in marriage and in communal life.[14]

[13] "There is one being execrated by all of Greece: Helen, for whom so many heroes were killed beneath the walls of Troy. Everyone wants to see her destroyed, just vengeance for so many misfortunes that followed her footsteps. But the gods decided differently; they save that abhorred woman. For Aeschylus, Helen was the symbol of desire, the Greek equivalent of the Oriental Maia" ("L'Oedipe à Colone et le culte des héros," pp. 27-28). Cf. E. T. Owen, *The Harmony of Aeschylus*, pp. 82-83. He calls Helen "the high priestess of Até."

[14] Apollo's argument in the trial is an effort to show why this difference is a necessary and therefore befitting state of affairs. According to a third century inscription, one of Apollo's maxims was, "Keep women under rule." Winnington-Ingram argues that Clytemnestra "hated Agamemnon, not simply because he had killed her child, not because she loved Aegisthus, but out of a jealousy that was not jealousy of Chryseis or Cassandra, but of Agamem-

Thus a fundamental theme of the *Oresteia* is the proper ordering of the marriage relationship. The trial of Orestes concerns
this institution within the city as well as the guilt of Orestes himself, for one of the consequences of the trial is a moral evaluation
of marriage. All who have broken the bond of marriage are punished and a new guardianship over the sacred relation of man
and wife is established. The avenging Erinyes are turned to this
task of overseeing the family:

> Death of manhood cut down
> before its prime I forbid:
> girls' grace and glory find
> men to live life with them.
>
> (*Eum.* 956-959)

So sing the Eumenides as they take their place by the hearth-
stone of houses in the city.

In the sacred covenant of marriage as a necessary foundation
to the welfare of the city lies the hope of the just commonwealth.
This has been made clear not only in the action of Clytemnestra
and the references to Helen, but also in the sufferings of the un-
fortunate Cassandra. The terrible punishment meted out to her
by Apollo is the result of yet another violation of the marriage
vows and female duty. She explains to the chorus of Argive elders
that Apollo took her as consort:

> CASSANDRA: Yes, then; he wrestled with me, and he breathed
> delight.
> CHORUS: Did you come to the getting of children then, as
> people do?
> CASSANDRA: I promised that to Loxias, but I broke my word.[15]
>
> (*Ag.* 1206-1208)

---

non himself and his status as a man. For she herself is of a manly temper,
and the dominance of a man is abhorrent to her. Thus when she kills her
husband, it is not only an act of vengeance, but also a blow struck for her
personal liberty" ("Clytemnestra and the Vote of Athena," p. 132).

[15] There is a problem of translation here which affects the interpretation
of the passage.

1207: ἦ καὶ τέκνων εἰς ἔργον ἤλθετον νόμῳ;
1208: ξυναινέσασα Λοξίαν ἐψευσάμην.

In breaking her word and denying her duty Cassandra violated the covenant of marriage. Apollo's punishment of her can be explained on these grounds, as can the fact that he, the god who according to legend has been frequently cheated by women, argues for the rights of the male and the sacredness of marriage.[16] His experience with both Coronis and Cassandra is that of a man whose right as father has been denied.[17]

Thus Apollo's dispute with the Erinyes in the trial scene is an effort on the part of the god to prove, on the basis of biological and social facts, that the male must rule, and the marriage rela-

----

1207: Came you also to the making of children, as the custom is?
1208: I gave my consent and then deceived Loxias.

Is Cassandra asserting that she denied her body to Apollo, or that she did accept him, but cheated him of the children he anticipated? Line 1206 would imply the latter. It may be that the ambiguity is due to a confusion of traditions. E. Bethe in *Homer, Dichtung und Sage* (Leipzig, 1914), suggests that the Cassandra legend existed in different forms, one of which said that Apollo bestowed the power of mantic divination in return for love; the other that Cassandra never accepted Apollo, and was in consequence killed by him. Whatever Aeschylus intended, there is no ground for asserting as Davreux does that "il faut renoncer à expliquer pourquoi, après tant d'héroïnes qui ont repoussé Apollon, Cassandre est la seule qui ait eu à subir de façon aussi complète les effets de la colère du dieu" * (Juliette Davreux, *La légende de la prophétesse Cassandre d'après les textes et les monuments*, "Bibliothèque de la faculté de philosophie et lettres de l'université de Liège," No. 94 [1942], p. 30). In the context of the *Oresteia* Cassandra's punishment is merited.

* "One must give up trying to explain why, after so many women have rejected Apollo, Cassandra is the only one who has had to bear so fully the consequences of the god's anger."

16 *Eum.* 213-224.

17 H. J. Rose overlooks the importance of the relationship between Apollo and Cassandra when he says, "Aeschylus is here doing no more than following the conventions of his day, which lay at the disposal of every teller of tales to use as he saw fit. For the purposes of his plot, Cassandra was literally loved by a literal god in bodily form; it is a tale which will make a good scene, and it does not suit his purpose here to reflect on its implications" ("Theology and Mythology in Aeschylus," *Harv. Theol. Rev.*, XXXIX [1946], 1-24). Not only is the incident of great importance in explaining why Apollo treats Cassandra as he does (otherwise it is a wanton act quite inconsistent with the role the god plays in relationship to Orestes), but it is one of the several themes which contribute to the final argument at the trial of Orestes. Without clearly understanding that Cassandra has violated a sacred covenant, both her position and Apollo's arguments appear meaningless.

tionship be steadfastly fixed through male domination. The positions which underlie the arguments advanced by Apollo and the Erinyes have been incisively stated by Hegel:

> [The Erinyes] enforce . . . the family right in so far as this is rooted in the blood relation. The profoundest association of son and mother is the substantive fact which they represent. Apollo opposes to this natural ethical relation, rooted as it is already both on the physical side and in feeling, the right of the spouse and the chieftain who has been violated in respect to the highest right he can claim. This distinction is in the first instance brought to our notice in an external way since both parties are champions for morality within one and the same sphere, namely the family. . . . The relation of children to parents reposes on the unity of the natural nexus; the association of man and wife on the contrary must be accepted as marriage, which does not merely proceed from the purely natural love, that is from the blood or natural affinity, but originates out of the conscious inclination, and for this reason belongs to the free ethical sphere of the self-conscious will. However much, therefore, marriage is bound up with love and feeling it is nonetheless to be distinguished from the purely natural emotion of love, because it also freely recognizes definite obligations quite independent of the same, which persist when that feeling of love may have ceased. The notion, in short, and the knowledge of the substantiality of marital life is something later and more profound than the purely natural connection between mother and son, and constitutes the beginning of the State as the realization of the free and rational will.[18]

Yet many readers have been struck more by the seeming absurdity of Apollo's argument than by anything else. If we understand why he argues as he does we can do away with the most formidable difficulty of the trial scene, and will then be in a position to comprehend the significance of Apollo in the action of the drama.

The argument between the Erinyes and Apollo turns upon two questions: 1) which is the more serious crime, the killing of a man by his wife or the killing of a woman by her son? 2) is the

---

[18] *The Philosophy of Fine Art,* tr. F. P. B. Osmaston (London, 1920), II, 214-15.

man or the woman the true parent of the child? [19] The answer to the second question will determine the answer to the first. The Erinyes, concerned only for violent acts between those related by blood, argue that Agamemnon and Clytemnestra were not related by blood, being man and wife, but that Orestes and Clytemnestra are so related. Hence they are obliged to hunt down and take the life of Orestes, while they had no interest in the murder of the king.[20] In answer to Orestes' question, "But am I then involved with my mother by blood-bond?" (*Eum.* 606), they answer, "Murderer, yes. How else could she have nursed you beneath/her heart? Do you forswear your mother's intimate blood?" (*Eum.* 607-608) Orestes turns to Apollo to answer this assertion. The god begins by describing the crime in all its horror: a great man, "lord of the host of ships," was chopped down by a scheming woman. This in itself is the greatest evil. But, answer the Erinyes, Zeus himself shackled his father; how then can Apollo speak for the father? Apollo points out that the gods do not kill—they are immortal and can undo what is done; but among men, once blood

[19] Winnington-Ingram points out that Clytemnestra emphasizes the close relationship between mother and child, as well as the father's role in procreation. She makes it clear that though the woman has as well-founded a claim as the man, the woman's position is inferior. Thus when Clytemnestra speaks of Iphigenia, "in each case the phrase is completed by words expressive of the father's share in the child. 'His own child, my dearest birth-pang' (*Ag.* 1417). 'My branch raised up by him' (*Ag.* 1525). . . . Thus both the offenses of which Clytemnestra accuses her husband are sins against marriage and strike at the status of the woman in marriage." The issue is raised again by Clytemnestra and Apollo. Apollo, "You pursue an offense by a child, but not an offense by a wife against her husband"; Clytemnestra, "You pursue an offense by a wife against her husband, but not an offense against a child" ("Clytemnestra and the Vote of Athena," pp. 135-36).

[20] The arguments at the trial are complicated by the fact that the Erinyes have a twofold function: they are, technically, the Erinyes of Clytemnestra, hence are interested only in offenses against her and would not be concerned with any other person. The Erinyes of Agamemnon, invoked by Electra and Orestes at his tomb, would be concerned to see he is avenged. The Erinyes are also used by Aeschylus as representative of blood-vengeance morality in general. Their arguments are at once personal and typical, as against the morality represented by Apollo. Cf. Hubert J. Treston, *Poine, a Study in Ancient Greek Blood Vengeance* (London, 1923), pp. 120f.

is spilled upon the ground there is no undoing. Yet, the Erinyes say, Orestes did just this with Clytemnestra; is he not to be punished for it? (*Eum.* 625-656) But, Apollo counters, Clytemnestra is not the parent of Orestes:

> I will tell you, and I will answer correctly. Watch.
> The mother is no parent of that which is called
> her child, but only nurse of the new-planted seed
> that grows. The parent is he who mounts. A stranger she
> preserves a stranger's seed, if no god interfere.
> I will show you proof of what I have explained. There can
> be a father without any mother. There she stands,
> the living witness, daughter of Olympian Zeus,
> she who was never fostered in the dark of the womb
> yet such a child as no goddess could bring to birth.
>
> (*Eum.* 657-666)

If Apollo is correct, the argument of the Erinyes has no validity and the evidence for the gravity of the two crimes points to the murder of Agamemnon by Clytemnestra as the more serious offense. More serious, that is, if it can be shown that though there is no blood crime there (Apollo and the Erinyes would agree that man and wife are not related by blood; all Apollo has shown is that both crimes are of the same kind: non-kin murders), there is a reason why a woman who murders her husband must be punished and why that offense is more serious than the act of Orestes. Here the argument leaves the biological realm and returns to the political, for note that Apollo concludes his argument on the role of the male in procreation by an appeal to Athena and her city:

> In all else, Pallas, as I best may understand,
> I shall make great your city and its populace.
> So I have brought this man to sit beside the hearth
> of your house, to be your true friend for the rest of time,
> so you shall win him, goddess, to fight by your side,
> and among men to come this shall stand a strong bond
> that his and your own people's children shall be friends.
>
> (*Eum.* 667-673)

This is followed by an address from Athena to the men of Attica who sit as the jury in the trial. She too argues on the need for political stability, order and justice in the *polis*. It is this issue which decides the judgment given, and to this we will return shortly.

Apollo's argument on the right and biological superiority of the male has called forth a variety of misunderstandings. Treston has maintained, as has Owen, that the argument is mere rhetoric, an absurd and meaningless effort to answer the Erinyes.[21] Greene, while recognizing that the argument used by Apollo presents a view "widely held in ancient Greece," still assumes that "the poet must have written with tongue in cheek, meeting the bad and partial argument of the Erinyes with one as bad and as partial.[22]

One critic, although taking the argument seriously, has not been able to place it in context as far as the over-all dramatic design is concerned. Solmsen writes:

> When Apollo urges the superior worth of the male sex, represents Clytemnestra's deed as much more hideous than Orestes', and finally supports his argument by a theory which makes the male partner of a marriage the real progenitor while the woman is merely the preserver of his seed, we must not allow ourselves to find here merely a bundle of sophistries and lawyer's tricks,[23]

and then adds in a footnote:

> I do not know whether the doctrine endorsed by Aeschylus was that which prevailed at the time nor whether it was the only one that

[21] Treston, *Poine*, p. 289: "He advances the absurd opinion that the real parent of a child is the father, not the mother." Owen, *The Harmony of Aeschylus*, pp. 114-16, 126-27: "But the poet is called upon to make an arguable case of it, and therefore has to supply a form of argument. Reply and counter-reply are needed to make good theater, from the Athenian point of view, and he thinks he can best give the dialogue the effective verbal play loved by his audience by sharpening it to a very definite point of debate."

[22] William Chase Greene, *Moira* (Cambridge, Mass., 1944), p. 135. He believes that Athena uses Apollo's argument as grounds for breaking the tie: "The tie vote of the Areopagus sufficiently dramatizes the impossibility of deciding the issue on such grounds as either the Erinyes or Apollo have taken; while the acquiescence of the impartial Athena with the principle put forward by Apollo at least provides a motive, however absurd, for her breaking the tie, though it also evades the moral issue." On the contrary, Athena does not evade the moral issue, but like Apollo uses the dominance of the male as factual evidence on which the moral issue must rest.

[23] *Hesiod and Aeschylus*, pp. 191-92.

he knew. In any case it seems a mistake to regard it as a σόφισμα dragged in to bolster up a bad case. Rather, I should think that Aeschylus felt satisfaction at finding physical theory at one with the comparative appraisal of the sexes which had been reached on political, ethical, or whatever grounds. . . .[24]

Finally, Winnington-Ingram suggests that the weight of Apollo's third argument is very difficult to assess for it follows upon two arguments which, he believes, are intended to be obviously absurd since Apollo is, he assumes, represented by Aeschylus as the spokesman for the Delphic morality, a half-way house between the primitive morality of the Erinyes and the enlightened morality of Athena. But he is not able to conclude that Apollo's third argument is in fact intended to be absurd. He writes:

> This argument has been the source of much perplexity. Clearly it performs one function in the play: it prepares the way for a compliment to Athena and for the part she is to have in deciding the verdict. But did Aeschylus take it seriously or mean his audience to do so? I cannot feel that either he or they would have regarded it as more than at the best an unproved speculation. Why then is it introduced? Because, unless some such theory should be true, there remains that fundamental inconsistency in the god's position. Were it true it would be the only completely valid argument that he could employ to justify the matricide.[25]

I believe it was intended seriously, and that it makes the previous two arguments less absurd than Winnington-Ingram believes they are.

Indeed, a great deal which is to be taken seriously lies behind the argument. But to experience its dramatic power, we must understand that the view expressed was widely held, and that there were certain biological beliefs supporting it, especially the belief that the male was established in his superior position by the nature of the procreative substance which only the male could transmit.

That this view was not peculiar to Aeschylus is indicated in sections of both Plato's *Timaeus* and Aristotle's *On the Genera-*

[24] *Ibid.,* footnote, p. 194.
[25] "The Role of Apollo in the *Oresteia,*" *Classical Review,* XLVII (1933), 97-104.

tion of Animals.[26] Plato associates seed with the marrow and the brain,[27] and asserts that the male transmits it from the brain and spinal column to the womb where it is nourished until the new creature is born.[28] Throughout the latter part of the *Timaeus* Plato implies that because of the structure of the human body, the male is the one responsible for the rational element with which offspring are endowed. In the male the "Eros of begetting" takes various forms, simple physical desire being but a lower manifestation of what in its most exalted form is the desire for wisdom. But the power of procreation is conferred upon man in order that the reasonable element in him may find future embodiments. Here, as in the *Oresteia,* biological and cosmological theories are of a piece.

Aristotle believed that the "male provides the form and the principle of the movement; the female provides the body, in other words the material. . . .";[29] that "the female provides the material, the male provides that which fashions the material into shape. . . . Thus the physical part, the body, comes from the female and the soul from the male since the soul is the essence of a particular body." [30] For Aristotle as for Plato the transmission of semen is the manner of passing on from one generation to the next a substance which, since it comes from the immortal part, the brain and spinal marrow, makes possible the typically human activity of reasoning. There is in the male something of the divine, the *logos.* Hence the male is closer to the gods. The Eros of the male is that daimon which enables men to contemplate the heavens and aspire to the pure state of knowing. The semen, since it comes from the brain where the daimon resides, is the immortal part of man which produces the striving after wisdom in the

[26] Similar views are to be found in various fragments of the pre-Socratic thinkers, but the remains are so slight that it is difficult to say more than that in all likelihood there was a tradition from which Aeschylus could draw. See the fragments of Hippon of Samos, Anaxagoras of Clazomenae, and Diogenes of Apollonia in Diels, *Die Fragmente der Vorsokratiker* (Berlin, 1937).

[27] *Timaeus* 73b-d, 91.

[28] *Timaeus* 90e-91d.

[29] *On the Generation of Animals,* I, xx, 729a (tr. A. L. Peck).

[30] *Ibid.,* 738b.

generated offspring. In addition, Aristotle maintains, the semen contains something divine, *pneuma*. The *pneuma*, he asserts, is foam-like stuff, more divine than the elements and analogous to the substance which makes up the stars. Thus the male possesses that which is eternal and unchanging.[31]

Further evidence for the Greek belief in the origins of life and the role of the male in procreation is given by Onians:

> There is this various evidence that the head is holy with potency by which to swear and make appeal and was thought to contain the life or ψυχή apparently in its actual contents, the 'εγκέφαλος, the somewhat uncanny brain and cerebrospinal fluid, 'the most peculiar of the parts' of the body as it appeared even to the scientific Greeks. ... So in the Iliad there is this curse, indicating it seems to me, that the brain fluid (the 'εγκέφαλος) is the semen; the life-giving fluid: "May the 'εγκέφαλος of themselves and of their children flow (ρέοι) to the ground even as this wine does and may their wives be mingled with other men." The brain was holy; not to be eaten. It had nothing to do with ordinary consciousness (perception, thought, and feeling being the business of the chest and its organs), but instead was the vehicle of life itself, of that which continues and does not die. But life does not merely persist in the individual; it issues forth and a new life begins. This is the greatest miracle, the holiest mystery. Elsewhere and ... in earliest Greece it was those parts of the body that were the seats and source of life in this sense that were revered, counted holy, so that men made appeal or oath by them. It was natural and logical to think that the 'life' or ψυχή issuing from a man must come from the 'life' or ψυχή in him, from his head therefore, and, helping that location, to see in the seed, which carries the new life and which must have seemed the very stuff of life, a portion of the cerebrospinal substance in which was the life of the parent.[32]

On biological grounds it can be demonstrated, then, that the male is the true parent, and on cosmological grounds it can be shown that the male, since he possesses semen, is capable of participating in the *logos* which is a manifestation of *nous*. Plato asserts that men are endowed with a slight part of *nous* which the

---

[31] *Ibid.*, 736a-737a.

[32] Richard Broxton Onians, *The Origins of European Thought* (2nd ed.; Cambridge, England, 1954), pp. 108-9.

gods have wholly, and it is *nous* which orders both the heavens in their perfect activity and the best kind of action in men.[33] Hence men can act more like the gods than can women, and men are the best equipped to rule the family and the city. Characterization of the women in the *Oresteia* suggests that Aeschylus shared the view later expressed by Plato, that the male is better able to rule since he is less subject to passion than the female, and endowed with the ability to judge rationally. So Apollo's argument for the moral superiority of the male is an effort to adduce biological evidence to convince those, especially women, who might question the male right. As Athena demonstrates shortly after Apollo's argument, the city must be ruled by reason and persuasion with enough fear mixed in to control the headstrong. Aeschylus applies this himself in placing in Apollo's mouth an argument which once and for all settles the question of who should rule by an appeal to incontrovertible facts.

The movement from one moral outlook to another demands, then, that a number of beliefs be firmly established, and in the trial scene both gods contribute to that factual foundation. But the gods function in the dramatic action not merely as philosophers whose job it is to tell the truth about the gods and about men; they are agents of moral enlightenment too, for they guide Orestes to the place where he is to be judged, and they determine what the new moral code is to be. In short, they lead Orestes out of his house into the city.[34]

As the god who prepares the way for Orestes' agony, Apollo is variously presented in the drama. He is first directly invoked when the herald returns from Troy with news of the victory. In

---

[33] Cf. *Timaeus* 47e-51e; *Philebus* 28c-31; *Laws* 875c-d. In connection with this see Cornford's epilogue in his translation of the *Timaeus*. In early mythological accounts, e.g., Hesiod's *Theogony*, the sky is male and the earth female. The female is associated with necessity and something irrational, while the male is associated with *logos* and the rational. It is from earth that the basest, most irrational, and violent creatures are born.

[34] Just as Agamemnon is lured into the house by Clytemnestra, there to be "judged" and condemned by the blood morality of a primitive family right overseen by the Erinyes, so Orestes is lured into the city by Apollo and Athena, there to be judged by a jury of citizens, the Areopagus, overseen by the morally enlightened Zeus.

that invocation the three grace-bestowing gods who ultimately
will effect Orestes' expiation are mentioned together: Zeus,
Apollo, and Hermes. Apollo, the most intimately involved with
Orestes' crime and subsequent purification, is a god who, as
Orestes says, understands "what it is to do no wrong" (*Eum.* 85-
86). Yet we see that he can exact the most awful vengeance upon
those who have wronged him, for Cassandra has been ruined by
his anger. While he would be remembered as one of the gods who
sided with the Trojans against the Achaeans, in the conclusion of
the trilogy he is presented as no longer provincial in his concerns.

As opposed to Athena, a local goddess, Apollo is panhellenic; [35]
he is the god who understands miasma and catharsis. This probably accounts for the fact that though he argues for Orestes, he,
unlike Athena, has no vote in Athens. His universal concerns prevent his participation in the immediate judicial functions of the
Areopagus, but do account for his aid to Orestes. Since Orestes
comes from a family in which crimes against both the Erinyes of
the individual family member and against gods of other localities
have been committed,[36] and since he has been liberated, through
his exile, from the limiting moral perspective of his own house
and city, he is particularly fitted to become the recipient of
Apollo's wisdom. Orestes has been led to see that the good is not
identical with the ancestral, that there is a law which transcends
local custom. It is this that Apollo argues for as against the spells
and incantations of the Erinyes.

But Apollo cannot bring Orestes to this new moral awareness
without the help of both Zeus and Hermes. Like Apollo, Zeus and
Hermes are gods who have become civilized. Their more primitive behavior serves as a background for this transfiguration, just
as the cities of Troy and Argos are used as the more primitive
early organizations of men which stand behind the Areopagus of
Athens. The moral development in the human order is a reflection of, indeed is made possible by, the moral development in the
community of the gods. The fight Zeus had to wage to establish

[35] Cf. W. K. C. Guthrie, *The Greeks and Their Gods* (London, 1950),
Ch. VII.
[36] *Ag.* 524-528.

his order on Olympus is the prototype for the war between Argos and Troy and the resolution of that war in Athens. The ruin of two cities ends in the greater achievement of a third. That Zeus can expedite this end is a firm belief of the chorus:

> Now to my supplication, Zeus,
> father of Olympian gods,
> grant that those who struggle hard to see
> temperate things done in the house win their aim
> in full.
>
> (*Lib. Bear.* 783-787)

The chorus also remembers the fate of the two older earthly communities:

> Justice came at the last to Priam and all his sons
> and it was heavy and hard,
> but into the house of Agamemnon returned
> the double lion, the double assault,
> and the Pythian-steered exile
> drove home to the hilt
> vengeance, moving strongly in guidance sent by the god.
>
> (*Lib. Bear.* 935-941)

Events are falling out in a pattern determined by divine counsel.

Finally, Hermes has been ennobled too, for he ceases to be merely the "comrade of dark night," the wily god of robbery, crafts, and dreams, and becomes the guide to Orestes in search of purification and just judgment. Hermes, the god of wayfarers, is adjured by Apollo to lead Orestes to that place sacred to Pallas Athena:

> Hermes, you are my brother from a single sire.
> Look after him, and as you are named the god who guides,
> be such in strong fact. He is my suppliant. Shepherd him
> with fortunate escort on his journeys among men.
> The wanderer has rights which Zeus acknowledges.[37]
>
> (*Eum.* 89-93)

[37] The cult and worship of Hermes is discussed in Farnell, *Greek Hero Cults and Ideas of Immortality*. Jane Harrison speaks of Hermes as "the very *daimon* of reincarnation" because of his role as *psychopompos* and his origin as a snake. He is the most appropriate guide for Orestes (*Themis,* p. 295).

The gods who have undertaken to guide Orestes are presented as acting from a new moral eminence. Just as Orestes faced Clytemnestra and defied her, so the sources of their consciences in the supernatural realm must face each other; Apollo and the Erinyes have either to come to a settlement or remain forever at war. We have been reminded from the first that a morality based solely on the family relationship is limited and contradictory. The *Agamemnon* closes on a note of confusion and alarm: although the Erinyes demand the revenge that has been taken, the chorus of elders cannot see that way of settling wrongs as just (*Ag.* 1560-1564). The play ends with the citizens and their leaders, Clytemnestra and Aegisthus, completely hostile toward each other. Likewise, the second drama ends with Orestes confused and distraught, for he cannot reconcile the two courses of conduct that are known to him. In the face of the conflict between the two orders of morality and their contradictory claims upon the individual, he goes mad.

If mortal man is to overcome a morality of blood revenge and realize a rational morality of political justice he requires divine aid, for the change is a fundamental one. In the human realm it is the achievement of rationality, symbolized in the drama by the purgation of Orestes and his return to sanity. Clarity of moral vision is achieved only by the intervention of Apollo and Athena who must demonstrate that reason has a place in moral decisions. And they do this by asserting that moral questions are not simply the concern of one man or one family; all of society is involved in them, and the development from a familial sense of obligation to a civil court of Athenian elders is a consequence of this fact. The promptings of Apollo and Athena in the Areopagus are the endeavors of rational man to control his passions; the revengeful accusations of the Erinyes are the expression of instinctual passion.

Yet the Erinyes, it must be emphasized, are representatives of an older generation of gods among whom strict moral laws obtained. It is wrong to see them as evil forces or as destructive of law; rather they support a system of morality, which is rigorous in its demands. They are, as H. J. Rose has said, "co-mates of Justice herself, embodying the wholesome fear which is needed to

restrain those who will not be righteous of their own accord." [38]
But the extent of wrongdoing that they are capable of considering
is limited, and they care nothing for wrongs between individuals
not related by blood. To what extent Aeschylus has given us his
own interpretation of the Erinyes and to what extent he follows
traditional views of them it is difficult to say. H. J. Treston has
distinguished several different views of the Erinyes and pointed
out that none of them exactly fits the presentation given by Aeschylus.[39] Comparing Aeschylus' treatment of the Erinyes with
Hesiod's, Solmsen points out that Aeschylus, who drew heavily
from Hesiod, has not followed the earlier writer in placing them
in the age of Uranus, but rather sees them as the daughters of
Night. It is also Aeschylus who "credits the older generation with
a law (*nomos*), an order." [40] The Erinyes, as Aeschylus presents
them, are representatives of a strict, lawful morality which goes
back to the very beginning of the created order. Hence the
Erinyes are not capricious and must be seriously dealt with. Solmsen writes:

> The Furies as conceived by Aeschylus are not always actuated
> merely by blood lust and blood thirst. They can rise above these
> motives and think of themselves as guardians of certain ethical
> principles whose maintenance is an indispensable condition for the
> existence of a moral and civilized society. . . . Their vigilance may
> parallel and supplement the work of the Areopagus; inasmuch as
> they are concerned with the so-called 'unwritten laws,' it may cover
> spheres in which positive law as such ceases to be effective.[41]

But there needs to be a clarification of both the unwritten as
well as the written law. This is achieved, at least by implication,
in the final trial, for there both the matters about which there
can be no legislation and the matters that can be dealt with by
written law are worked out. The first is dealt with in the clarification of what is required of the individual to be morally enlightened and just in his conduct; the second is dealt with in the de-

[38] "Theology and Mythology in Aeschylus," *Harv. Theol. Rev.*, XXXIX
(1946), 1-24.

[39] *Poine*, pp. 120ff.

[40] *Hesiod and Aeschylus*, p. 183.

[41] *Ibid.*, p. 199.

termination by Apollo and Athena of what constitutes the just city. The first will be discussed briefly here in terms of the growing moral awareness of the individual as reflected in the case of Orestes. The second will be discussed in the next chapter as part of the whole question of law and the city.

The fact that the Areopagus comes to replace the Erinyes is a reflection of a similar substitution which occurs in the development of the individual. The moral development of the civilized individual is from a primitive instinctual mode of behavior dominated by passion to a restrained conduct ruled by reason. Yet this is achieved, just as the Athenian knowledge of justice is achieved, only through controlling and changing the function of passion. If the Erinyes are cast out altogether and not recognized for the code of conduct they stand for, they will return and wreak a horrible revenge.[42] So too in the individual, if the claims of passion are not recognized, actions done from seemingly rational motives can become perverted and reason can be used to the most irrational ends.

But the primitive morality, represented by the Erinyes, is difficult to overcome. As the early history of the house of Atreus testifies, the old morality encourages unbridled expression of violence. The desire for revenge is freely satisfied as long as there is a sense of an overriding moral demand outside the individual that must be satisfied. The way of blood revenge is conceived of as the way men *ought* to behave, but this way is dictated by powerful external forces: the individual is not personally responsible for his actions because he is dominated by forces greater than his will or conscience. Morality is thus "legalized" but the lawgiver is not the individual or his community of wise men but the daimonic powers of the supernatural—in other words, the irrational side of man, not his reason.

The daimonic supernatural forces are specific in their commands: their voices speak with urgency in the present instant; they allow no time for deliberation. They do not permit questions, and thus when a man like Orestes who has traveled, who has been instructed by an enlightened teacher, questions the an-

[42] *Eum.* 779-786.

cestral ways, he discovers inconsistencies in the moral obligations set forth. The morality which enjoins blood retribution appears to be irrational to him. Therefore he cannot exult in his act [43] as his mother could when she took the life of Agamemnon. While Clytemnestra celebrates her deed as if she too is one of the Erinyes made strong by blood, nourished by murder, Orestes seeks first to rationalize his act and then appeals to Apollo for help:

> But while
> I hold some grip still on my wits, I say publicly
> to my friends: I killed my mother not without some right.
> My father's murder stained her, and the gods' disgust.
> As for the spells that charmed me to such daring, I
> give you in chief the seer of Pytho, Loxias. He
> declared I could do this and not be charged with wrong.
> Of my evasion's punishment I will not speak:
> no archery could hit such height of agony.
> And look upon me now, how I go armored in
> leafed branch and garland on my way to the centrestone
> and sanctuary, and Apollo's level place,
> the shining of the fabulous fire that never dies,
> to escape this blood that is my own.
>
> (*Lib. Bear.* 1025-1038)

Orestes' moral confusion stems not only from the fact that he must perform an action repulsive to his nature, but also from the fact that he has been commanded to perform it by Apollo, who is himself opposed to the ancestral morality of the Erinyes and is himself the overseer of purification. Orestes assumes that the discipline of the god implies abstention from impulsive action; yet Apollo's words must be heeded. There is no doubt that what he commands is wrong. It remains for the trial to demonstrate that it is not as serious as the act committed by Clytemnestra, and that Orestes can be declared not responsible for it. While he *is* guilty, for he did commit the act knowingly, he can be purified and reconciled with the community.[44]

---

[43] "My victory is soiled, and has no pride" (*Lib. Bear.* 1017).

[44] J. H. Finley argues, as I do, that Orestes is responsible for the act of matricide. "It is clear," he writes, "that Aeschylus so deeply feels a man's responsibility that he rejects the thought of evil as originating in a man's

It becomes evident as the action proceeds that Orestes will learn from Apollo and Athena what he dimly realizes before their help is received: rational morality enjoins the individual to refrain from action until the *right* of action has been established. The right of action is realized through considerations which go far beyond the individual's impulses and desires; the individual and the family, the house and the clan become subordinate to the city.

But the right of action cannot be expressed merely in injunctions of the sort given by the Erinyes who command "Thou shalt—," who assert specific acts in retaliation for wrongs the individual has sustained:

> You must give back for her blood from the living man
> red blood of your body to suck, and from your own
> I could feed, with bitter-swallowed drench,
> turn your strength limp while yet you live and drag you down
> where you must pay for the pain of the murdered mother,
> and watch the rest of the mortals stained with violence
> against god or guest
> or hurt parents who were close and dear,
> each with the pain upon him that his crime deserves.

> (*Eum.* 264-272)

In a rational morality the right must be determined by deliberation and the springs of conduct molded through persuasion. It is the deliberative and persuasive conditions for rational morality that are dramatically presented in the action of Orestes' trial.

Such a distinction between blind commandments and deliberative acts resting on the choice of the reasonable man has also been noted by Plato who is concerned with many of the same problems that appear in Aeschylus' writings. Thus in the *Laws* Plato draws

---

ancestors rather than in himself. Clytemnestra later seeks to excuse her crime on the ground that she is precisely such an agent of the past, but though the chorus recognizes this element in her action, they passionately refuse to deny her own responsibility." And, "by admitting the evil with the necessity of his act, Orestes at last shows a moral awareness of what he is doing, a freedom from the automatism of hurt and counterhurt. . . . He knows that his act is one of atonement as well as of vengeance, and the Furies whom he now begins to see do not come to him quite against his will or by surprise" (*Pindar and Aeschylus*, "Martin Classical Lectures," XIV [1955], 258-59, 272-73).

a distinction between laws and the necessary "preludes" or "preambles" to laws. The function of the preludes is to give a reasonable explanation for the law so that a rational man can understand the arguments behind the specific injunction.[45] The law is coercive, the prelude is persuasive and if the latter fail in its function the former must be invoked and adherence to it enforced. Thus Plato asserts that "as we chant this prelude to those who purpose these unholy deeds, destructive of civic life, the law itself we must leave unvoiced for him who obeys; but for him who disobeys we must suffer the law, following on the prelude. . . ." [46] The Athenian Stranger's purpose as legislator is to make the preludes to the laws available to the young, without stating the law itself, so that the soul of the citizen will be formed in accordance with justice, and the grounds for good conduct will be known. But should the individual lack the aptitude for self-control in accordance with the preludes, he is to be punished by the laws without explanation. In the first case, where rational action follows on understanding of the moral exhortations, the individual controls himself; in the second case, where the law itself is laid down and enforced, the individual is coerced into a certain pattern or suffers the penalty for an act "because the law says thus and so." Now this differentiation in the grounds of action is similar to the two moralities represented by the younger gods and the Erinyes.

The displacement from individual to community is possible

[45] Cf. *Laws* 718b, 722d-723b: "All utterances and vocal expressions have preludes and tunings-up (as one might call them), which provide a kind of artistic preparation which assists towards the further development of the subject. . . . The part which we called the 'despotic prescription'—comparing it to the prescriptions of the slave doctors we mentioned—is unblended law; but the part which preceded this, and which was uttered as persuasive thereof, while it actually is 'persuasion,' yet serves also the same purpose as the prelude to an oration. To ensure that the person to whom the lawgiver addresses the law should accept the prescription quietly, in a docile spirit—that, as I supposed, was the evident object with which the speaker uttered all his persuasive discourse. Hence, according to my argument, the right term for it would be not legal 'statement,' but 'prelude,' and no other word. . . . The lawgiver must never omit to furnish preludes as prefaces both to the laws as a whole and to each individual statute" (tr. Bury).

[46] *Laws* 854c-d (tr. Bury). Cf. *Laws* 871.

only as a concomitant to a reformed view of the springs of human
action and human responsibility. When the agent acts in terms of
a morality based on unrestrained impulses, he sees his action (as
does Clytemnestra) as given justification by a force outside of and
greater than himself.[47] In the *Oresteia* the potency of this outside
force is attested to by the Erinyes' role in the crimes of the house
of Atreus. Their terrifying, vindictive purpose is seen by Cassandra:

> Now I will tell you plainly and from no cryptic speech;
> bear me then witness, running at my heels upon
> the scent of these old brutal things done long ago.
> There is a choir that sings as one, that shall not again
> leave this house ever; the song thereof breaks harsh
> with menace.
> And drugged to double fury on the wine of men's
> blood shed, there lurks forever here a drunken rout
> of ingrown vengeful spirits never to be cast forth.
> Hanging above the hall they chant their song of hate
> and the old sin; and taking up the strain in turn
> spit curses on that man who spoiled his brother's bed.
>
> (*Ag.* 1183-1193)

The forces at work are greater than the ability of the individual
to stay them; he is, under these circumstances, suffering passion
in the sense that he is impotently passive. The forces of revenge
work through him and are not under his control. This feeling of
passivity is clearly articulated, for several of the speeches refer to
the accumulated force of wrong which overwhelms the individual,
the family, and at times the whole city. The thirst for blood that
is aroused in men is like the wild lion in the young cub. The
chorus in the *Agamemnon* sings of it:

> But it grew with time, and the lion
> in the blood strain came out; it paid
> grace to those who had fostered it
> in blood and death for the sheep flocks,

[47] Both Aeschylus and Plato recognize that many individuals can be
"tamed" to participate in the *polis* only if their behavior is restrained through
fear, that is, through the coercion of both laws and edicts of supernatural
origin. This will be discussed in the following chapter.

a grim feast forbidden.
The house reeked with blood run
nor could its people beat down the bane,
the giant murderer's onslaught.
This thing they raised in their house was blessed
by God to be priest of destruction.

(*Ag.* 727-736)

The image so successfully used in this passage has relevance to
every situation in the drama in which wrongdoing has led to the
destruction of the perpetrator. The house of Atreus has nurtured
a lion in its midst; the Danaans who sailed against Troy have let
bestial violence grow among them until, with the destruction of
the city and its altars, they have brought death to their enemy
and themselves.

Yet for the individual who can only realize actions in terms of
powerful external forces which overwhelm reason there is a protection in this view of human guilt. If the forces of evil and retribution act through the individual the responsibility for action can
be placed outside; supernatural, or at least non-human, forces are
to blame. Orestes is unable to place the blame outside himself, for
his conscience seeks its integrity in viewing violence as the willed
action of men. Inspiration and guidance may come from the gods,
but the responsibility rests with the individual. This is why
Orestes' willingness to do what Apollo has directed is an act of
acceptance and faith. His faith in Apollo is vindicated by the outcome of events; but when he returns to avenge his father's death
he cannot know how they will turn out. Thus he enters the city of
Argos and later the city of Athens with fear and hope; he assumes
the "ingrown vengeful spirits" must be satisfied, but he does not
understand how they can be subdued. Apollo and Athena give
him this last great wisdom.

Through the trial in the Athenian law court they demonstrate
how a man may be judged by his fellow men and need not be
judged by the shades of the departed and the chthonian powers.
Thus the law court establishes in the city the power of rational
judgment which Orestes had attempted to exercise in regard to
his own actions. The community of men is to help the individual

when he has chosen badly and stands in need of judgment. With the use of reason men living together in the city can become the judges of what is right. They can come to distinguish *expiation* and *reconciliation* for the guilty citizen.

The two views of human action represented by the Erinyes and Apollo maintain two different ways of bringing the man who has committed a wrong back into the city. The more primitive blood morality requires expiation of guilt; the more enlightened political morality requires reconciliation of the guilty one while admitting the guilt. Thus the Erinyes cannot admit a man back to the family hearth unless he is guiltless. One who is guilty must suffer the extreme penalty: death or, equally final, separation from the gods of his domestic religion.[48] But Apollo, the god of purification, can receive a man once he recognizes his wrong and is purged of the evil tendency even though he remains guilty of having committed a wrong. Apollo and Athena show the citizens of Athens that a man can be received back into the community even though he is responsible for taking the life of a member of his own family.

This is one consequence of placing responsibility for action in the individual rather than in daimonic powers outside the individual. In this respect the development of moral awareness in Orestes has a significance that goes far beyond his individual case. When a man becomes responsible for his acts because he tries, insofar as he can, to be ruled by reason, he becomes subject to the judgments and determinations of his fellow citizens so far as they too act rationally. Thus he opens the way for reconciliation with

[48] Cf. Coulanges, *The Ancient City*, Ch. XIII. The exclusively familial concerns of the Erinyes contrast with the concern for justice on the part of the new gods. Aeschylus presents the radical difference between the gods who inhabit the hearth and those whose domain is the cosmos. He, like the early philosophers of Ionia, is inquiring into the place of the gods. "We can easily understand," writes Coulanges, "that for the ancients God was not everywhere. If they had some vague idea of a God of the universe, this was not the one whom they considered as their providence and whom they invoked. . . . The exile, on leaving his country behind him, also left his gods. He no longer found a religion that could console and protect him; he no longer felt that providence was watching over him; the happiness of praying was taken away. All that could satisfy the needs of his soul was far away" (p. 200).

his fellows if he commits a wrong, for reason can decide matters of punishment and degrees of guilt, as well as the fitness of a man to be received back into the community.

When men act irrationally, and are incapable of deliberative judgment, reconciliation is not possible; then guilt requires expiation, and that is realized only if a penalty is paid: the individual must cease to be guilty. But a man, like Orestes, who has taken the life of a member of his family, can never cease to be guilty. As long is he did commit the act it is wrong and requires retaliation since there is no rational agency to determine means and ends appropriate to the special circumstances and the motivation of the guilty man.[49] Hence he can only cease to be guilty by becoming the object of revenge himself; he needs to be subjected to that which he imposed upon another and reconciliation is impossible. The Erinyes would hunt Orestes down regardless of his motives and disposition. On the other hand Apollo, recognizing the conditions of action and the state of the agent, would declare Orestes fit to re-enter the community of men even while recognizing Orestes' guilt. Retribution is not the only way to deal with wrong. But such a view, maintained by the new gods, is possible only if certain necessary conditions are realized: the ordering and control of primitive impulses by reason, the knowledge of the cosmos as intelligible, and the establishment of law and justice in the *polis*.

These conditions can be represented in various ways, and in the *Oresteia* there is at least one complete statement of their fulfillment. Tragic drama was for the Greeks one means of stating these conditions; philosophy was another. Each provides a commentary on the other in certain limited respects; within each there are fundamental concepts that provide a structure for action and argument. The following two chapters will consider a few of these crucial ideas.

[49] Cf. *Laws* 874e-875d where it is pointed out that, although injustices can be committed under laws allowing no exceptions, laws are necessary in the absence of a wise lawgiver and statesman.

CHAPTER FOUR

LAW, RULE, AND THE POLIS

Who has the right to speak on the subject of rule and states-manship? Who can legislate for men living in cities? Who speaks truly about what is best and where happiness is to be found? Aeschylus' contemporaries would have regarded him, the poet in-spired by the divine, as one who could tell the truth about such matters, and therefore one who can put into the mouths of gods what it is right to say. The gods most knowing about cities and men are Apollo and Athena, the two who inspire the most reliable human teachers, poet and philosopher. Athena speaks as the di-vine statesman, one who knows the ways of legal institutions and the necessary role of fear in controlling unruly citizens. Apollo speaks as the inspirer of poets, himself a poet, one who knows the ways of purification and story to cleanse and teach men.[1] Both are to be understood as practitioners of art in the broadest sense: art as the process of making, which requires knowledge and technical competence. Both are educators who can teach the inhabitants of cities to live justly and well; as divine teachers Apollo and Athena can be accepted, for the words they speak are in accordance with the decrees of Zeus.[2]

But among men, those who teach as philosophers and poets cannot be so readily accepted, for human knowledge is limited and human wisdom rare. We know that the Greeks asked who can be trusted in such matters, and answered the question in dif-ferent ways. Some took the poets as moral and political leaders; others distrusted the poets and turned to professional statesmen, either tyrants, or Sophists, or to teachers such as Socrates. Plato's dialogues present us with an imaginative reconstruction of such questions and disputes. Plato argued that there was this similarity in the activities of the poet and the statesman: both were working

[1] Cf. *Laws* 653d-654. "Education owes its origin to Apollo and the Muses."
[2] *Eum.* 614-621, 796-799.

63

as artists, makers, who created something in accordance with a model and succeeded insofar as they came close to its perfection; both failed when what was created turned out to be a mere phantasma, a poor imitation, rather than an imitation in the real sense of a copy of what is perfect.[3]

Insofar as the poet and the philosopher know the original nature of the things they represent and talk about, they can be trusted; and it seems to be the case that both Aeschylus and Plato took seriously the role of poet and philosopher as teachers, especially as teachers of political wisdom. Certainly the *Oresteia* speaks authoritatively about matters of human action and civil rule: the serious drama of this type can articulate truths about a great variety of things crucial to the welfare of the state. Further, it represents these truths by means of music, dance, speech, action, and the other accompaniments of theater which are themselves means of education.

The drama as a possible way of stating the truth is given its philosophical justification and critique after Aeschylus has become established as an inspired teacher whose memory is venerated by many Athenians. No better example of the kind of drama Plato both feared and admired can be found than the *Oresteia*. In the *Laws* Plato comes to the conclusion that the tragic poet and the statesman are doing similar kinds of work, that is, providing a representation of the best life; and in addition achieve this by means of disciplines which are themselves conducive to self-control and modesty. In Book II, for example, he gives a defense of the Dionysiac chorus.[4] "In our view," the Athenian Stranger sums up, "choristry as a whole is identical with education as a whole." And further, tragic drama as a whole is identical with statesmanship as a whole. "Most excellent of

[3] In the *Sophist* an analysis of "art" is given. At 236a-c and at 266d Plato distinguishes between εἰκαστική and φανταστική. The first is good image-making and produces things like the original. The second is bad image-making and produces something which seems like the original but is really a mere semblance. Cf. *Laws* 667d-669b. Cornford discusses this problem in *Plato's Theory of Knowledge* (New York, 1957). For a precise analysis see J. Tate, "Plato and 'Imitation,'" *Classical Quarterly*, XXVI (1932), 161-69.

[4] *Laws* 667d-674c.

strangers," the Athenian says to tragic poets who might wish to dwell in the city he is planning, "we ourselves, to the best of our ability, are the authors of a tragedy at once superlatively fair and good; at least, all our polity is framed as a representation of the fairest and best life, which is in reality, as we assert, the truest tragedy. Thus we are composers of the same things as you yourselves, rivals of yours as artists and actors of the fairest drama, which, as our hope is, true law, and it alone, is by nature competent to complete." [5] The tragic poet will be admitted to the city and given a chorus by the rulers provided he can prove that his utterances are the same as those of the lawgiver. But since, as Plato points out, the truest tragedy is completed only by law, it would follow that in his view the statesman, since he understands the meaning of law and the right laws to draw up, would be by and large better fitted to serve as tragedian than the poet. Yet the poet Aeschylus does function as a lawgiver and statesman, for he consciously represents, through the utterances of the actors in his drama, the laws for the city which will make it the guardian of the best life for men. Presumably Plato's statesman would provide Aeschylus with a chorus.

The view that tragedy is a serious representation of matters pertaining to justice in the city is held by both Aeschylus and Plato. The *Oresteia,* like Plato's *Republic* and *Laws,* is not intended as "mere entertainment," but as serious education whatever else it may have been intended to provide. It is concerned to exhibit both just and unjust lawmakers, evil and beneficent rule, as part of the tragic action. It is first of all a drama, but one that takes political matters with the utmost seriousness.

The most obvious evidence for this contention is the trial scene in the *Eumenides.* The chief action here is shared by the two advocates for the defense, Apollo and Athena. The former defends Orestes prior to the ballot and leaves after the vote is taken, for his job is finished. Athena remains to bestow civil order on a people divided on the question of Orestes' guilt. The tie vote of the Athenian citizens is indicative of an ethical and political fact: among men there will always be divided allegiance to the de-

[5] *Laws* 817b-c (tr. Bury).

mands of ancestral morality and to the demands of political morality. The well-being of the *polis* requires that political morality
override the ancestral, and that the latter, though it cannot and
ought not be extirpated, be at least controlled by the statesman
who must see to it that the ways of the family do not frustrate the
ways of the city.

Athena's tie-breaking vote for the acquittal of Orestes is evidence that the gods favor the city over the family. The establishment of the tribunal, made up of citizens of different families, is
itself a means of overcoming an individual's concern for what is
merely his own. Athena explains to the citizens that she establishes the tribunal so that the city of Athens may prosper and
excel all others in political wisdom.[6] Further, she explains that
the seat of justice is to be henceforward the hill of Ares where
once the Amazons encamped against Theseus and were vanquished.[7] Although the *Oresteia* was probably written some ten
years before the Parthenon was started, it is clear that the role of
Athena in that drama and her role as depicted on the metopes
which adorned the Parthenon is the same: in both she stands as
the divine spokesman for the cosmic moral order; in both she
champions a moral law backed by her father, Zeus. And both
works of art see the triumph of Athens over her enemies as paral-
leling the triumph of the new gods over the old.[8]

In making Athena the founder of the Areopagus, Aeschylus
has found a way to vindicate his conception of its extended re-
sponsibilities. While originally the Areopagites were guardians
of prescribed ancestral ritual and the rules for dealing with de-
liberate homicide, Aeschylus depicts them as responsible for the
unbiased application of law according to an ideal of civil justice.
Their enlarged moral function is paralleled by the greater scope
and depth that Aeschylus conceives for the drama. This growth,

[6] *Eum.* 700-706.
[7] *Eum.* 681-690.
[8] The metopes were concerned with four themes: the battle of the gods
and the giants (at the front); the battle of the Lapiths and Centaurs; the
battle of Greeks and Amazons; the fall of Troy. Although Athena's statue
stood in the cella, a statue of Zeus was given the place of honor in the eastern
pediment. For a discussion of the structure and adornment of the Parthenon,
see C. J. Herington, *Athena Parthenos and Athena Polias* (Manchester, 1955).

part of reason's work in civilizing the community, is exhibited in the movement from the first to the third part of the trilogy. The typical drama of revenge is followed by a drama in which violence is pondered by reason. Artistic form and legal process evolve together. Events in Troy and Athens are seen as two kinds of trial:

> Indeed the frequent use in the *Agamemnon* of terms having a strong legal colouring makes it by no means unlikely that Aeschylus pictured the Trojan war in one aspect as a legal process for punishing the wrong done by robbery, ἁρπαγή, and theft, κλοπή, of Helen. The Atreidai are treated as joint claimants, ἀντίδικοι, with equal rights against the man who had abused the hospitality given him. But their expedition was seen by the brothers as directly commissioned by the gods after divine consideration and vote, the judgment, however, like the arguments, being manifested by the sword rather than by words. To this extent the gods are claimed to have been collaborators with the two kings in the defeat of Troy.[9]

The gods collaborate in a second legal action, this one founded on a matured conception of justice, when Orestes faces the accusations of the Erinyes.

Athena's opponents in the trial of Orestes are the Erinyes whose view of statecraft differs in some fundamental respects from her own. But they are not forced to argue their case with her until after they have encountered Apollo. A comparison between the ways in which Apollo and Athena argue with the Erinyes will show that among the gods descended from Zeus there is a progressive movement toward the realization of Justice, for Athena carries further and modifies the rigid requirements of Apollonian morality. Since both are guided by and speak on behalf of Zeus, it can be inferred that Aeschylus wishes to represent Olympian morality as itself the working out of an adequate morality of the *polis*. The Erinyes, Apollo, and Athena are each representative of stages in this evolution.[10]

[9] J. Walter Jones, *The Law and Legal Theory of the Greeks* (Oxford, 1956), pp. 249-50.

[10] This view is supported by R. P. Winnington-Ingram in "The Role of Apollo in the *Oresteia*." In brief his argument maintains that Zeus is represented by Aeschylus as a god who has lived through a number of moral revolutions, each one a reflection of his attempt (since he is the author of events)

When the arguments are considered in the order of their moral adequacy we approach more and more closely to a true view of Justice. It is as if we, the audience, are to be allowed a vision of Justice as Zeus has approximated it in his search for the true nature of Dike. Is it far-fetched to believe that this sort of search and discovery is what Plato had in mind when he described the ascent of the man of wisdom from mere opinion to true knowledge, and what he meant when he said the true tragedian is like the statesman? Both the Aeschylean and Platonic conceptions of Deity assert that god can be defined as the consciousness which knows reality, i.e., the form of Goodness and Justice. Where they differ is in the evolutionary element; Plato asserts that the gods have ever been as they are now; Aeschylus that even Zeus had to come to know, through a kind of divine inquiry, what the nature of Justice really is.

It is clear that Apollo is arguing for the male and is himself representative of the force and dominance of the male, while the Erinyes argue for the female. Apollo uses two modes of attack against them: one is insult and castigation, the other argument based on fact. In both instances he would cast them out entirely. Thus he first attacks them with invective:

> The repulsive maidens have been stilled to sleep, those gray
> and aged children, they with whom no mortal man,
> no god, nor even any beast, will have to do.

---

to approximate the true nature of justice. Thus Zeus is himself to be regarded as the power responsible for an evolution in morality. In this light the *Oresteia* is seen as the story of the search for and discovery of justice on the part of Zeus who communicates his knowledge through Athena. But Zeus has also inherited a moral system from a primitive time prior to his accession to power. That system has gone on functioning despite his search for a truer justice. It is as if a benevolent king were to ascend the throne following the rule of an unjust tyrant. He might find his people living unjustly, and they might continue to do so even while he worked out a more just polity. Thus the Erinyes go on functioning at the same time that Zeus is working toward the true nature of justice. Apollonian (or Delphic) morality is an important step toward the morality represented by Athena, but still not sufficient. Yet the ultimate moral outlook retains elements of its predecessors. Note that neither the Erinyes nor Apollo claim descent from Dike, but Dike (according to Hesiod) sits on the right hand of Zeus. Perhaps for Aeschylus Dike has taken the place of Moira in the earlier (especially Homeric) writings.

It was because of evil they were born, because
they hold the evil darkness of the Pit below
Earth, loathed alike by men and by the heavenly gods.

(Eum. 68-73)

And accuses them of committing unjustified bloody acts:

This house is no right place for such as you to cling
upon; but where, by judgment given, heads are lopped
and eyes gouged out, throats cut, and by the spoil of sex
the glory of young boys is defeated, where mutilation
lives, and stoning, and the long moan of tortured men
spiked underneath the spine and stuck on pales.

(Eum. 185-190)

But when the Erinyes demand that they be heard, "My lord
Apollo, it is your turn to listen now," he answers them not by
argument to prove them wrong, but simply by stating that they
contradict the way of Zeus, Hera, and Aphrodite:

You have made into a thing of no account, no place,
the sworn faith of Zeus and of Hera, lady
of consummations, and Cypris by such argument
is thrown away, outlawed, and yet the sweetest things
in man's life come from her, for married love between
man and woman is bigger than oaths, guarded by right
of nature.

(Eum. 213-219)

The Erinyes cannot be persuaded by Apollo, and he simply dis-
misses them by warning that they will suffer for what they do
(Eum. 222-234). In this first encounter Apollo has merely asserted
that he stands for a moral order sanctioned by an ultimate cosmic
intelligence, while they stand for an order that is at best limited
because irrational and contrary to the established order of things.

However, Apollo does not use this kind of argument when he
faces the Erinyes at the trial, but rather reverts to an argument
which meets the Erinyes on their own ground: namely, that the
mother is no true parent but the father is, and therefore the
father deserves first consideration. It has been pointed out that
this argument is an effort to establish on factual biological
grounds a position that assumes more than the right of the male:

the necessity to make the family subordinate to the city and to invest the prerogatives of statesmanship in the man rather than the woman because the male possesses capabilities for rationality that the female does not.

The contrast between "masculine" and "feminine" is clearly drawn by the behavior of Apollo and the Erinyes. The former is without moderation: he would destroy and cast out the Erinyes if he could; the latter are without moderation, but in another way: they would control men through fear and irrational appeals to blood ties. Apollo would control men through the power of the new order of gods, i.e., by way of Delphic morality which possesses more enlightened rules of conduct, but is completely lacking in the necessary element of persuasion.

Contrasted with these two immoderate ways of dealing with the problems of political morality is the way represented by Athena who exhibits the perfect mating of the male and female principle: she will argue for the right of the male as the rational, properly ruling one, and will respect the female claim. Upon the latter she will exercise her understanding of moderation and her art of persuasion.

Athena combines the best of both male and female, namely, courage and moderation.[11] Athena deals with the Erinyes far differently from Apollo, for she recognizes the need to accept the ancestral claim upon men:

> Yet these, too, have their work. We cannot brush them
> > aside,
> and if this action so runs that they fail to win,
> the venom of their resolution will return
> to infect the soil, and sicken all my land to death.
> > (*Eum.* 476-479)

Her arguments, like Apollo's, take two forms, but one of them is based upon persuasion, a technique of moderation unknown to the male god. Her first argument, after the Erinyes and Apollo

---

[11] Contrasted with her, quite forcefully because of the way Aeschylus handles the two characters, is Clytemnestra who combines the worst of both male and female, namely foolhardiness and irrational excess.

have been heard, declares that she is for the male, certainly a position that appears unjust:

> It is my task to render final judgment here.
> This is a ballot for Orestes I shall cast.
> There is no mother anywhere who gave me birth,
> and, but for marriage, I am always for the male
> with all my heart, and strongly on my father's side.
> So, in a case where the wife has killed her husband, lord
> of the house, her death shall not mean most to me. And if
> the other votes are even, then Orestes wins.
>
> (*Eum.* 734-743)

Now Athena's seemingly unjust preference for the male is in fact her attachment to what is right by nature, ordained by Zeus and necessity, and her disengagement from the ancestral. For she associates the male with nature and reason, the female with the unnatural and irrational.[12]

Having stated her position Athena, guided by the inspiration of Peitho, must bring the Erinyes into the city. Here her proper role as statesman is revealed. And at first she speaks much as the Erinyes do, of the need to keep fear in the city; on this point she can speak openly before her opponents. But what she recognizes, which they do not, is that the city can survive and achieve justice only if the restraint of fear is established by the reasonable power of law.

[12] Note the way the Erinyes are described by the Pythia at the opening of the *Eumenides*. Later, in their complaint to Athena, they are allied with the primitive forces of Earth and Night that ruled before the cosmic evolution that brought the younger gods into ascendency. They are part of the primordial order following upon chaos that existed before the present time; and they are related to the destructive inhuman forces which chaos was supposed to have spawned. On this point J. H. Finley notes that the Pythia gives "the divine model of earthly evolution. When she staggers from the temple in horror at the Furies it is as if she had recognized with shock an unsuspected residue in the world which had not shared this evolution" (*Pindar and Aeschylus*, p. 277). Still further significance may be found in the opening scene. It may be that the presence of the Erinyes in the shrine of Apollo is intended to cast doubt on his competence as a moral teacher—his house is itself defiled. Perhaps its intent is to ask, "How fit is Apollo morally to perform this function of expressing the will of Zeus?" (Winnington-Ingram, "The Role of Apollo in the *Oresteia*").

The Erinyes point out that fear is a necessary instrument of control:

> There are times when fear [τὸ δεινὸν] is good.
> It must keep its watchful place
> at the heart's controls. There is
> advantage
> in the wisdom won from pain.
> Should the city, should the man
> rear a heart that nowhere goes
> in fear, how shall such a one
> any more respect the right?

(Eum. 517-525)

And Athena answers in words which at first seem identical:

> Thus
> I advise my citizens to govern and to grace,
> and not to cast fear [τὸ δεινὸν] utterly from your city. What
> man who fears [δεδοικὼς] nothing at all is ever righteous? Such
> be your just terrors, and you may deserve and have
> salvation for your citadel, your land's defence,
> such as is nowhere else found among men, neither
> among the Scythians nor the land that Pelops held.
> I establish this tribunal.

(Eum. 696-704)

This warning is first of all a move in the effort to effect reconciliation between the Erinyes and the City where justice is to rule, and secondly a plea for fear based upon "just terrors," not the irrational fears which the Erinyes would use to control men. Athena agrees with the Erinyes that fear is necessary, but has a rather different conception of fear than they do. Her conception of the fear necessary to control the citizens of the *polis* is a part of the moderation and persuasion which she is to exercise in winning over the Erinyes. For in winning them over she makes the fear they would instill in the hearts of men no longer operative: the Erinyes become guardians of fertility for the city, and their former vengeful role is given up. What then can Athena mean by the fear that guarantees righteousness? [13]

[13] The word for fear used by both the Erinyes and Athena is τὸ δεινὸν which has the connotation of a response to what is terrible, dread, awful because remarkably strong and powerful; hence a power greater than man, per-

The fear she refers to is purposefully engendered by the wise lawgiver. It embraces a variety of emotions intended to promote civic virtues, such as shame, respect for the city and its laws, modesty in action, and fear of the just vengeance of the gods. The Erinyes, if they were allowed their way, would instill an animal-like, congenital fear, a brutish fear of inherited guilt and capricious fate.

Plato has drawn the distinction in the *Laws* between the fear that derives from insecurity about the future, the forces of nature and death, and the fear instilled by the just lawgiver in persuading men that they ought to regard the laws as sacred and live justly.[14] The former rests on the fear of pain, adverse for-

---

haps something supernatural. But Athena also uses the verb $\delta\epsilon\iota\delta\omega$ ($\delta\epsilon\delta o\iota\kappa\grave{\omega}s$) which is to be distinguished from $\phi o\beta\epsilon\omega$, and connotes fear that is less strong, more responsible than that experienced when $\phi o\beta\epsilon\omega$ and its variants are used. Earlier (690-691) Athena speaks of the hill of Ares upon which Athens is founded as guarded by the reverence ($\sigma\epsilon\beta as$) and fear ($\phi\acute{o}\beta os$) of the citizens. Now $\sigma\epsilon\beta as$ connotes shame which is aroused in one who contemplates doing something disgraceful. So Athena is aware, as the founder of the city, that the citizen must feel a fear out of reverence for the moral commands of the divine and the law of the city. The Erinyes would provoke fear based on their direct vengeful actions which have not the support of divine reason. Men can only properly honor and fear what is ultimately reasonable. Athena assures the Erinyes that her actions are in accord with the "luminous evidence" of Zeus. Cf. Plato *Epistle VII* 336d-337.

[14] *Laws* 646e ff. (tr. Bury).
Ath. Tell me now: can we discern two kinds of fear, of which the one is nearly the opposite of the other?
Clin. What kinds do you mean?
Ath. These: when we expect evils to occur, we fear them.
Clin. Yes.
Ath. And often we fear reputation, when we think we shall gain a bad repute for doing or saying something base; and this fear we . . . call shame.
Clin. Of course.
Ath. These are the two fears I was meaning; and of these the second is opposed to pains and to all other objects of fear, and opposed also to the greatest and most numerous pleasures.
Clin. Very true.
Ath. Does not, then, the lawgiver, and every man who is worth anything, hold this kind of fear in the highest honor, and name it "modesty"; and to the confidence which is opposed to it does he not give the name "immodesty," and pronounce it to be for all, publicly and privately, a very great evil?
Clin. Quite right.

tune, suffering, the latter on the fear of breaking the laws because they are just. The former is irrational, the latter rational fear. The former, both Plato and Aristotle agree, must be purged, and is initially dealt with, they maintain in the *Laws* and the *Politics,* by music, dance, gymnastics, and the arts. The latter is a necessary prerequisite for political justice, and on that account is conscientiously fostered by the wise statesman who knows that only through fear for the laws themselves can the majority of men be governed.[15] This kind of fear can be justified because it rests on what is in accordance with human nature. That is to say, it is the only workable substitute for rational understanding, when that is lacking; but it can be replaced by reason, and is in the case of those whose intellectual ability is sufficiently acute to grasp the truth about human society.

Since such men are few in number, and since most men suffer from an unpatriotic, atavistic fear, the preservation of the city depends upon exorcising fear and inducing shame in the citizens. Although the latter is a kind of fear, namely fear of contravening the laws, it has a positive effect in the courage it provokes, for if one fears to break the laws he becomes courageous in the defense of his city and righteous in his behavior. Shame, then, is the emotion which the statesman uses to counteract that primordial fear which is further exorcised by the art of choristry in the broadest sense.[16]

Ath. And does not this fear, besides saving us in many other important respects, prove more effective than anything else in ensuring for us victory in war and security? For victory is, in fact, ensured by two things, of which the one is confidence towards enemies, the other, fear of the shame of cowardice in the eyes of friends. . . . Moreover, when we desire to make a person fearless in respect of a number of fears, it is by drawing him, with the help of the law, into fear that we make him such.

[15] Cf. *Politics* VIII, 4-7. On the need to fear, *Nic. Ethics* III, 6 (tr. Ross): "Now we fear all evils, e.g., disgrace, poverty, disease, friendlessness, death, but the brave man is not thought to be concerned with all; for to fear some things is even right and noble, and it is base not to fear them—e.g., disgrace; he who fears this is good and modest, and he who does not is shameless" (1115a 10-14).

[16] The sociological interpretation of religion so often met among classical writers followed from the belief that fear was an essential means to controlling the citizens. For example, Sextus Empiricus, *Against the Physicians,* I.54

Athena intends to use the guardianship of the Erinyes as one means of inducing the proper kind of fear; they are offered "a place of your own, deep hidden under ground . . . where you shall sit on shining chairs beside the hearth to accept devotions offered by your citizens." [17] They will be the goddesses concerned with the sanctity of the marriage tie.[18] They are persuaded by Athena to take over the concern for men and women living together in the family which Apollo had, in his immoderate way, tried to administer. They too will act as a restraining force on those who, lacking shame and modesty, try to place themselves above the good of the community. Athena urges them:

> No, let our wars range outward hard against the man
> who has fallen horribly in love with high renown.
> No true fighter I call the bird that fights at home.
> *(Eum.* 864-866)

And they promise her that they will guarantee civil tranquility:

> This my prayer: Civil War
> fattening on men's ruin shall
> not thunder in our city. Let
> not the dry dust that drinks
> the black blood of citizens
> through passion for revenge
> and bloodshed for bloodshed
> be given our state to prey upon.
> *(Eum.* 976-983)

The power of persuasion has won the ancient goddesses over to a support of the new order:

> I admire the eyes
> of Persuasion, who guided the speech of my mouth
> toward these when they were reluctant and wild.

(tr. Bury): "Critias [was one of the atheists who claimed that] the ancient lawgivers invented God as a kind of overseer of the right and wrong actions of men, in order to make sure that nobody injured his neighbors privily through fear of vengeance at the hands of the Gods." See also Polybius, *The Histories,* VI, 56.

[17] *Eum.* 804-807.

[18] *Eum.* 835.

Zeus, who guides men's speech in councils, was too
strong; and my ambition
for good wins out in the whole issue.

(Eum. 970-975)

As the founder of cities, Athena has a final deposition to make
in regard to the women who inhabit Athens. They, as the ones
to be ruled by men, must have their appointed place and their
proper duties. Athena calls upon the women of Athens, "maidens,
wives, elder women" to accompany the Eumenides to their abode,
for these together will watch over the city's well-being.

When the drama ends the city has been properly organized and
its rules ordained. The house has its gods of marriage, and the
city its gods of law and justice. The family has been brought to
its proper place in the city as the city has found its place in the
cosmos. Lawfulness has been established throughout. This lawfulness is not realized merely by divine fiat; it becomes possible
only when certain conditions are realized. They are: in the city,
control of passion by reason; in the universe, intelligible order.

The treatment accorded the Erinyes by Athena is recognition
of the fact that the irrational side of human nature must be controlled; it is the counterpart to the goddess' establishment of the
Areopagus.[19] Athena recognizes that it is not enough to found a
deliberative body to sit in judgment upon the wrongdoings of
citizens, for rational decision is only approximated. Men, when
serving as jurors, will be swayed by the claims of ancestral right

[19] According to Aristotle, *Athenian Constitution* XXV, the Areopagus was
done away with by Ephialtes about seventeen years after the Persian War,
i.e., about 462. The *Oresteia* was produced about 458. Hence the drama may
have had as one of its aims the re-establishment of the Areopagus, or at least
a body to act as *nomophylaces* in the traditional sense. See Martin P. Nilsson,
Cults, Myths, Oracles and Politics in Ancient Greece (Lund, 1951), Ch. III.
J. Walter Jones, *Law and Legal Theory of the Greeks,* Ch. VI. Good discussions of Athenian constitutional law and its evolution are in C. Hignett, *A
History of the Athenian Constitution to the End of the 5th Century B.C.*
(Oxford, 1952), especially p. 217; p. 263, note 156; p. 269, note 206. Also,
H. T. Wade-Gery, "Eupatridai, Archons, and Areopagus," *Class. Quart.,* XXV
(1931), 1-11, 77-89; "Studies in the Structure of Attic Society: I. Demotion-
idai," *ibid.,* 129-43; "Studies in the Structure of Attic Society: II. The Laws
of Kleisthenes," *ibid.,* XXVII (1933), 17-29.

and kin relationships, as the divided vote of the Areopagus demonstrates. The ties of blood will be honored, for the affections of human nature cannot be denied, in fact must be recognized as having a rightful place, subservient to reason, yet necessary as a force effecting the commands of reason. To deny the Erinyes, as Apollo would, is to send them into a kind of limbo from which they threaten to wreak horrible revenge. The tie of blood which they formerly represented is put to the necessary service of preserving the love between man and woman who come together to found the family. The family and the city now rest upon the affections which the Eumenides protect; and while these tendencies are irrational, they are also the motive power for a passionate concern for the well-being of men. In short, virtue can be achieved only if both νοῦς and θυμός are properly balanced; that is, the "restrictive understanding" and the "expansive desire" (to use Bruno Snell's interpretation of the terms) must be in harmony. The consequence of such order is σωφροσύνη (moderation) as opposed to ὕβρις (immoderate action). It guarantees control of excessive passion which can lead to the iniquities of the sort exhibited by the house of Atreus. But now when reason is overcome by passion there is within the city a court of justice to sit in judgment. This court shall judge according to law, that law which functions as restraining reason to restore the order of reason to the city.[20]

The second condition which makes possible Athena's organization of the city is the ability to understand the rationality of the cosmos. Law can exist for the city only when reason dominates men and is seen as part of the cosmic intelligibility. It is a far cry from the gods of Hesiod's *Theogony* to the categories of Aristotle's *Organon,* just as it is a far cry from the kinship morality of the Erinyes to the political morality of Athena. When nature can be conceived of as intelligible, human action can be so conceived as well. When nature is considered unintelligible, controlled by

[20] Cf. *Laws* 957c-d (tr. Bury): "For of all studies, that of legal regulations, provided they be rightly framed, will prove the most efficacious in making the learner a better man; for were it not so, it would be in vain that our divine and admirable law (νόμος) bears a name akin to reason (νοῦς)." Also, *Laws* 714a.

animistic forces which war among themselves, mankind too will be thought of as influenced, even controlled, by forces wholly outside his own nature. Therefore morality becomes something external, dictated by non-human forces, rather than internal, dictated by that reason in man which is a bit of the reason found throughout the cosmos. As nature is discovered to have its proper order and system according to law, so human activity can be seen to have its proper order and system under law. Nature and human conduct are reasonable. Just as the philosopher comes to distinguish accident and cause in nature, so man in the city comes to distinguish accident and responsibility in human behavior. Consequently moral rules can find their proper place in the conscience, as part of reason, within man.[21]

But the realization that the universe is intelligible brings about a new attitude toward and evaluation of the gods. It is this effort to reassess traditional theology that leads both Aeschylus and Plato to present the gods in a new light, for the achievements of human reason must needs be expressed in theology as well as science and art.

Only a new telling of old tales, only a reconstruction of old beliefs can make the civilization of the city-state a permanent achievement. The moral revolution among the gods which, as Aeschylus claims, has made Zeus supreme, the eternal ruler of the universe, must be mirrored in the moral revolution among men. Men see their way more clearly for having "witnessed" the moral revolution in another realm, yet their city, unlike Olympus, can never be permanently safe from the forces that threaten to dissolve it. As Plato warns at the conclusion of the *Laws:*

> But in every case, the full end does not consist in the doing, establishing or founding something: rather our view should be that it is only when we have discovered a means of salvation endless and complete, for our creation, that we are at length justified in believing

[21] Cf. Plato *Timaeus* 51e. The distinction between ancestral morality and right according to nature is part of the general distinction between *nomos* and *physis* which was of great concern to Greek philosophy. E. R. Dodds touches on this problem in *The Greeks and the Irrational* (Berkeley, 1951), p. 182.

that we have done all that ought to be done: until then, we must believe, the whole of our creation is incomplete.[22]

The city must strive to establish the same permanence in its organization that has been discovered to obtain in heaven. That is Athena's purpose, and she announces that it has been accomplished by means of "measures I have laid down/into the rest of time." [23]

In the *Oresteia* the new cosmic order, ruled over by Zeus, is in fact the objectification and counterpart of the long struggle toward justice that the Greek city had to undergo. But the old order remains, even though shackled in Tartarus. Zeus and the statesman must maintain eternal vigilance lest the forces of barbarism free themselves.

The conclusion of the *Oresteia* in fact states the conditions for the triumph of civilization over barbarism. The secret of that achievement lies in the use of reason which can both restore the individual to sanity and found a community like Athens. The clarity with which this is exhibited in the *Oresteia* is the reason why it can be called a complete work of art: there is a profound resolution of the central problem. Since the just society rests on self-control and self-knowledge, the suffering of Orestes is truly the universal condition of the individual who painfully arrives at wisdom, just as the story of Troy, Argos, and Athens is the universal story of civilization as the Greeks accepted and honored it.

We are now in a position to inquire further into the relationship of the lawmaker and statesman to the gods. It is obvious from the *Oresteia* that in the mind of Aeschylus religion and law are closely linked. When we better understand how he may have conceived that relationship we can go on to consider the place the poet as legislator may have had in the city of Aeschylus' thoughts.

The organization of the *polis*, its institutions and laws, can be in accord with divine sanctions. Should it fail to realize its proper

[22] 960b-c (tr. Bury).
[23] *Eum.* 572. See F. Vian, "Le conflit entre Zeus et la destinée dans Eschyle," *Revue des études grecques*, LV (1942), 190-216.

constitution as part of the divine order it must suffer decline, warfare, and eventual extinction. But there are many kinds of state constitutions which men may devise for themselves. While it became a problem for the Greeks to determine whether the *polis* existed in accordance with divine laws or by man-made conventional laws, certainly for Aeschylus there was no question about the fact that only through congruence with divine order could the constitution be called just. Whether or not the *polis,* which must be ordered in accordance with law, could ever achieve perfection is a question not specifically raised by Aeschylus, though it is, of course, dealt with at length by both Plato and Aristotle. But by the time of the great philosophical thinkers the problems of politics had become more critical and a whole school of both Sophists and natural philosophers had raised serious objections to the view that the city and its laws were of divine origin. The very existence of laws in the realm of human organization posed a serious question: could laws ever be the instrument of an ideal form of rule? Both Plato and Aristotle answer in the negative; since there can be no ideal law, there can be no ideal state. There can only be better and worse kinds of states, and one job of the political philosopher is to distinguish the various kinds and evaluate them.

Plato makes the point that the best kind of government would be one under a divinely inspired statesman, but since that is impossible we must be content with the second best, namely rule by means of law. The shortcomings of that kind of organization are clearly set forth in the *Statesman.* There the Stranger asserts that "in one sense it is evident that the art of Kingship does include the art of lawmaking. But the political ideal is not full authority for laws but rather full authority for a man who understands the art of Kingship and has kingly ability." [24] The best ruler would not rule by means of law for "law can never issue an injunction binding on all which really embodies what is best for each: it cannot prescribe with perfect accuracy what is good and right

[24] *Statesman* 294a (tr. J. B. Skemp). Cf. *Laws* 874e-875d.

for each member of the community at one time." [25] Thus law becomes like "a self-willed, ignorant man who lets no one do anything but what he has ordered and forbids all subsequent questioning of his orders even if the situation has shown some marked improvement on the one for which he originally legislated." [26] The best rule, then, would be of the sort which, we are told in the *Laws,* at one time existed when Cronus "appointed as kings and rulers for our cities, not men, but beings of a race that was nobler and more divine, daimons." [27] Now man can come closest to the rule by divine god-like beings if he is obedient to the immortal element within him, namely reason (*nous*), and lets reason rule by law which is proved close to reason by its etymological similarity (*nous* and *nomos*).[28]

It has been frequently pointed out that law for the Greek cities was complicated and confused because old and new statutes, both assumed to be divinely inspired, remained in force even though at times contradictory. When Plato argues that the laws must have a divine sanction and be in accord with the will of the gods [29] he is trying to redeem a past so remote as to be mythological—a past whose ideal unity was disintegrated by the growth of a complex society and by the development of naturalistic philosophies which hastened the general weakening of religion in the city. Since the ancient beliefs remained they led to confusion within the legal codes that were relied upon. Coulanges writes:

> In principle, the laws were immutable, since they were divine. It is worthy of remark that they were never abrogated. Men could indeed make new ones, but the old ones remained, however they might conflict with the new ones. . . . Written or unwritten, these laws were always formulated into very brief sentences, which may be compared in form to the verses of Leviticus, or the slocas of the book of Manu. . . . These ancient verses were invariable texts. To change a letter of them, to displace a word, to alter the rhythm, was

[25] *Ibid.* 294b.
[26] *Ibid.* 294c.
[27] *Laws* 713d (tr. Bury).
[28] *Laws* 714. The same comparison is made at 835d-e.
[29] *Laws* X.

to destroy the law itself by destroying the sacred form under which it was revealed to man. The law was like prayer, which was agreeable to the divinity only on condition that it was recited correctly, and which became impious if a single word in it was changed.[30]

With the growth of the city and legal institutions the challenge to religious and ancestral tradition became serious; a method for replacing outmoded laws with new ones had to be devised. In the late fifth century a technique of adjudication was worked out through a committee of *nomothetai*. "Before a new law came into effect," J. Walter Jones writes, "any existing law at variance with it had first to be expressly repealed, and it was in such a case of conflict between new and old laws that the Athenian attitude to legislation came out clearly. For the existing law must first be arraigned in a γραφή or prosecution 'against an independent law' brought in the popular courts by the sponsor of the new law and defended by advocates, σύνδικοι or συνήγοροι, some at least of whom were nominated by the assembly." [31]

These different attitudes toward the law are implied in the argument between Athena and the Erinyes. There is no precedent for overruling the Erinyes even though there may be other traditions to which appeal can be made. The problem in the trial of Orestes is to work out a way whereby contradictory laws can be mediated so that just judgment results. If the rule of the city were in the hands of Athena it would be the best possible in Plato's sense, for then decision appropriate to each case could be rendered without the need of law. But Athena establishes the Areopagus which, while divinely inspired and guided, is not capable of the absolutely just and individually right decisions of a god. When the gathering of Athenians must decide the right in this case they, representative of attitudes in the community at large, maintain both points of view: the claim of the Erinyes and the claim of Athena get equal recognition in the tie vote. It is then

[30] *The Ancient City*, pp. 190-91. In the *Laws* Plato puns on the words νόμος (law) and νόμος (chant, tune). In this double sense choristry can be the best education, i.e., it develops in the young grace and harmony while teaching and making known the laws. Cf. *Laws* 800, 817b-c, 700b, 722d, 734e. Also, Nares Chandra Sen-Gupta, *The Evolution of Law*, Ch. IX.

[31] J. Walter Jones, *Law and Legal Theory of the Greeks*, p. 109.

Athena's prerogative as the spokesman for Zeus to decide on ultimate grounds known only by the gods. She claims in making
this decision that she is acting in terms of what is absolutely right,
not what is seemingly right. She accuses the Erinyes of wishing
"to be called righteous rather than act right." [32] And after the decision is made she tells the Erinyes that she is acting from intelligence given her by Zeus and in accordance with his just decrees.
She therefore makes a distinction between what appears to be
right and what is right absolutely because of divine, not human
or ancestral, origin. The order she has established is the best representation in the city of the justice which holds throughout the
cosmos, while the order the Erinyes would perpetuate is at best a
feeble and distorted imitation which only appears to be right,
but in fact is not.

The final disposition of Orestes' case is thus taken to be just in
an ultimate sense; he receives just judgment because he is brought
to trial in a city where the gods have set up the best kind of government for men. This in fact is the conclusion of the political
theme in the *Oresteia* which has previously exhibited several
kinds of city rule.

The conclusion of the *Agamemnon* sees the establishment of a
tyranny at Argos, for Clytemnestra and Aegisthus must rule by
force.[33] Although Clytemnestra does not want any further violence
within the city, she threatens to force the citizens to obedience:

[32] *Eum.* 430.

[33] Lines 844ff. make it clear that under Agamemnon the rule was not to be
autocratic, for he asserts on his return:

> we will set a day
> For assembly [πανηγύρει] and debate among our citizens.

Virginia Woods Callahan, in *Types of Rulers in the Plays of Aeschylus* (Dissertation, Chicago, 1944), has noted that the "lines imply that the business
of the kingdom is carried on in a general assembly." This is contrasted with
a senate to which reference is made by Clytemnestra in line 884. Agamemnon
promises to rule with the advice of his people. He will not be like an oriental
despot, but like a physician who burns and cuts away the diseased parts:

> where disease wants remedy
> Fire or the knife shall purge this body for its good.
>
> (*Ag.* 849-850, tr. Vellacott.)

> But I say to you:
> go on and threaten me, but know that I am ready,
> if fairly you can beat me down beneath your hand,
> for you to rule; but if the god grant otherwise,
> you shall be taught—too late, for sure—to keep your place.
>
> (*Ag.* 1421-1425)

Aegisthus, with his usual bravado, promises the citizens that they shall feel his wrath:

> Still with this money I shall endeavor to control
> the citizens. The mutinous man shall feel the yoke
> drag at his neck, no cornfed racing colt that runs
> free traced; but hunger, grim companion of the dark
> dungeon shall see him broken to the hand at last.
>
> (*Ag.* 1638-1642)

Fear born of the armed might of the tyrant shall control the dissatisfied citizens of Argos.

At the conclusion of the *Libation Bearers* the city is divested of rule. While Orestes, who has killed the tyrants, is by the custom of ancestral right the one to assume the position of authority, he has committed a murder and must be judged before he can assume any prerogatives in the city. Unlike Clytemnestra and Aegisthus who forcibly take over the control of the city, he cannot rule unless it is with the consent of the gods, so that when he is established as the ruler he can claim to be ordained by the gods. This ordination, however, is unlike Agamemnon's which followed from the right of descent in the ruling family, and unlike Clytemnestra's which followed from the use of force. Orestes' rule will be that of the enlightened and taught statesman. The restoration of order in the city which the citizens await at the close of the *Libation Bearers* is accomplished by means of the events which take place in Athens. From this point of view Orestes' trial is like a lesson in statesmanship.

We can now understand why it is appropriate for Athena to determine the issue. She is indeed the example of the best statesman, for she accomplishes within the city what the gods (in this case, particularly Zeus) have accomplished throughout the universe. Statesmanship is one of the arts at the command of the divine craftsman. While Plato and Aeschylus disagree on the mythological background of present-day society, it is likely that they do agree in their views of what is best in the political realm, and the relationship that it ought to maintain to the cosmos. Aeschylus implies that the present social order is a definite improvement upon what went before, while Plato asserts that present-day society is a less adequate, debauched form, of a previous golden age.[34] Yet both Plato and Aeschylus seem to agree on the worth and justice of the court of law. Surely what Athena establishes in Athens is a deliberative body which is to sit in judgment on all kinds of cases. The goddess does not assert that laws can be formulated which would be as good as the just decisions of this body. And Aeschylus is of course optimistic and excessively nationalistic in pretending that the Areopagus could always remain free from corruption. It could, yes, if the gods always participated in the trials, as they do in the case of Orestes. But in fact they do not. Because of this fact, because men must govern themselves, laws are needed as themselves guides to the judges. Plato has expressed his view of this problem very well in the *Laws*, where as a prelude to laws concerning cases of death, he makes this pronouncement:

> It is really necessary for men to make themselves laws and to live according to laws, or else to differ not at all from the most savage of beasts. The reason thereof is this,—that no man's nature is naturally able both to perceive what is of benefit to the civic life of men and, perceiving it, to be alike able and willing to practise what is best. For, in the first place, it is difficult to perceive that a true civic art necessarily cares for the public, not the private interest,— for the public interest binds States together, whereas the private interest rends them asunder,—and to perceive also that it benefits both public and private interests alike when the public interest, rather than the private, is well enacted. And, secondly, even if a man

[34] Cf. *Laws* 679c, 680, 713, 714. There is one myth that presents the opposite view. In the *Protagoras* 322-323, it is said that men at first could not live together well, that Zeus sent Hermes to bring the art of statesmanship to men, and that he directed Hermes to implant a little of the art in all men. But this itself leads to trouble since now all men think themselves fit to rule.

fully grasps the truth of this as a principle of art, should he after-
wards get control of the State and become an irresponsible autocrat,
he would never prove able to abide by this view and to continue
always fostering the public interest in the State as the object of first
importance, to which the private interest is but secondary; rather,
his mortal nature will always urge him on to grasping and self-
interested action, irrationally avoiding pain and pursuing pleasure;
both these objects it will prefer above justice and goodness, and by
causing darkness within itself it will fill to the uttermost both itself
and the whole State with all manner of evils. Yet if ever there should
arise a man competent by nature and by a birthright of divine
grace to assume such an office, he would have no need of rulers over
him; for no law or ordinance is mightier than Knowledge, nor is
it right for Reason to be subject or in thrall to anything, but to be
lord of all things, if it is really true to its name and free in its inner
nature. But at present such a nature exists nowhere at all, except
in small degree; wherefore we must choose what is second best,
namely, ordinance and law, which see and discern the general
principle, but are unable to see every instance in detail.[35]

Now Athena's decision is to stand as a kind of law for the people
of Athens, telling them that in cases of this kind, should they
come up again, the death of the husband shall be counted as more
serious than the death of the woman who is his wife. This kind of
law can be relied upon because it is promulgated by the gods.
Every human law should come as close as possible to divine decrees. To argue this position requires that men believe the gods
exist and are just. Aeschylus makes that assumption. But Plato,
being a philosopher who is arguing a position against other views
(those of the Ionian materialists and the Sophists in particular)
must prove that the theology behind his political view is sound.
Therefore Book X of the *Laws* is in fact a theological argument
which stands as the most general, inclusive prelude to all of the
specific laws and their preludes.

Analogously, Aeschylus' theological assumptions provide a
"prelude" to the dramatic action of the *Oresteia*. All three of the
plays begin with prayers; all three invoke the divine order to
watch over the unfolding of events. The prelude to the search
for the best possible order in statecraft, whether carried out in

[35] 874e-875d (tr. Bury).

philosophical or dramatic terms, is theology. What the theology maintains, and the rational structure of cosmic and political law which it implies need to be considered.

There are two problems here: the place which religion ought to have in the life of the city, and the content of the religious beliefs. Both Aeschylus and Plato would agree that religion is a most important force in the life of the city but that it can no longer exist as a worship within the confines of the house and hearth. When Athena leads the Eumenides to their abode, their "places of eminence beside Erechtheus," [36] she conducts them to a shrine beneath the city itself, as guardians for the whole, hence no longer to be worshiped and propitiated privately as had been the case when Clytemnestra and Electra invoked them. Athena insists that the ancestral form of religious observance in which the house is the sacred place give way to the political forms of religious observance in which the city is the guardian of the gods. Likewise, Plato concludes his discussion of the being and nature of the gods with the insistence that no family or individual shall possess a shrine of its own. Thus one of the laws shall state:

> No one shall possess a shrine in his own house: when anyone is moved in spirit to do sacrifice, he shall go to the public places to sacrifice, and he shall hand over his oblations to the priests and priestesses to whom belong the consecration thereof; and he himself, together with any associates he may choose, shall join in the prayers. This procedure shall be observed for the following reasons: It is no easy task to found temples and gods, and to do this rightly needs much deliberation; yet it is customary for all women especially, and for sick folks everywhere, and those in peril or distress . . . and conversely for those who have had a slice of good fortune, to dedicate whatever happens to be at hand at the moment, and to vow sacrifices and promise the founding of shrines to gods and demi-gods and children of gods; and through terrors caused by waking visions or by dreams, and in like manner as they recall many visions and try to provide remedies for each of them, they are wont to found altars and shrines, and to fill with them every house and every village, and open places too, and every spot which was the scene of such experiences. . . . and a further reason is this—to prevent impious men from acting fraudulently in regard to these mat-

[36] *Eum.* 855.

ters also, by setting up shrines and altars in private houses, thinking to propitiate the gods by sacrifices and vows, and thus increasing infinitely their own iniquity whereby they make both themselves and those better men who allow them guilty in the eyes of the gods, so that the whole state reaps the consequences of their impiety in some degree—and deserves to reap them.[37]

Both Aeschylus and Plato would establish a cosmic religion which places the city above the family; and both would use the new religion as a control over the citizens. Fear, reverence, modesty, shame, obedience, piety, appropriate measure in conduct, and justice are the virtues they expect the religion of the *polis* to promote. Athena assumes that it will inculcate these virtues, and the *Oresteia* closes on a note of hopeful, joyful expectancy, for Athena, by the use of the intelligence granted her by Zeus, and by the power of persuasion has brought the new religion to birth.

Plato, as we know, could not be as optimistic as Aeschylus even though he generally agrees with the latter's political and religious point of view. Plato's consideration of the same problems provides a useful and penetrating addendum to the conclusion of the *Oresteia*. While the *Republic* would found the state upon rational philosophical grounds and use religion as a necessary adjunct to the wisdom of the philosopher, the *Laws* suggests that a religious foundation to the state is essential, but one which coexists not with the wisdom of the statesman who can rule without law, but rather with the structure of law itself. Thus the state Plato proposes in the *Laws*—a constitutional theocracy, something very like that presented by Aeschylus in the *Oresteia*—is second best, but the only really workable one.[38]

The laws necessary to the state must be carefully formulated by a wise man—a philosopher—but they are to take shape in accordance with the power of mind which resides in the universe and in the individual human being. That is, the construction of the *polis* on the part of the statesman is analogous to the construction of the cosmos by the demiurge as recounted in the

[37] *Laws* 909e-910b (tr. Bury).

[38] The plays of Aeschylus, especially the *Oresteia*, were often produced in the fourth century. See T. B. H. Webster, "Fourth Century Thought and the *Poetics*," *Hermes*, LXXXII (1954), 294-308.

Timaeus. But in the case of the statesman the material to be dealt with is not matter in the universe but rather human nature, certainly just as intractable as matter, and more dangerous because apt to get out of control. While the cosmos is set and ordered once and for all by the divine craftsman the political order of the city can easily degenerate into tyranny or democratic chaos.

Granting that the statesman's laws are good ones, the following means are to be used to maintain compliance with them. First, the lawgiver, like Athena, must rely upon persuasion. But persuasion cannot always be successful, so that the laws must be backed by force, if necessary. There are two reasons why force is essential: (1) only by force can the order of the city be kept in the face of inevitable attacks on it by irrational and selfish individuals; (2) only by absolute adherence to law can the *polis* come close to the divine order of the cosmos. A good constitution is an approximation of the best and true constitution which is that laid down by a real (i.e., semi-divine) statesman employing the true art of statecraft. Plato implies that no human constitution can ever exactly duplicate the best, but it comes closer to it, even in its deficiencies, when it demands and receives absolute obedience. Thus he asserts in the *Statesman,* "there is only one constitution in the true sense" [39] and all actual constitutions come closer to or fall further away from this ideal. While the true statesman can be directed by his art alone without the need to pay attention to laws, the average ruler and the mob he rules must abide by laws. This requirement, to meet the needs of the actual political situation, is discussed in the *Laws:*

It is, in a sense, a shameful thing to make all those laws that we are proposing to make in a state like ours, which is, as we say, to be well-managed and furnished with all that is right for the practice of virtue. In such a state, the mere supposition that any citizen will grow up to share in the worst forms of depravity practised in other states, so that one must forestall and denounce by law the appearance of any such character, and, in order to warn them off or punish them, erect laws against them, as though they were certain to appear, —this, as I have said, is in a sense shameful. But we are not now

[39] 297d (tr. J. B. Skemp).

legislating, like the ancient lawgivers, for heroes and sons of gods, when, as the story goes, both the lawgivers themselves and their subjects were men of divine descent: we, on the contrary, are but mortal men legislating for the seed of men, and therefore it is permitted to us to dread lest any of our citizens should prove horny-hearted and attain to such hardness of temper as to be beyond melting. . . .[40]

Since mortals are not gods and heroes, their constitutions will not be copies of the best. Hence, "it seems to follow that there is an invariable rule which these imitative constitutions must obey if they mean to reproduce as far as they can that one real constitution, which is government by a real statesman using real statecraft. They must all keep strictly to the laws once they have been laid down and never transgress written enactments or established national customs." [41]

But how can one be sure the written enactment is a just one? It was noted that the statesman stands to the city as the demiurge stands to the cosmos. In both cases the order established depends upon mind or reason, and art. To give a full explanation of why the parallel is justified and how mind and art combine to the end of producing the best, Plato requires that several presuppositions be laid down about the nature of the gods. Religious beliefs of a certain kind are prerequisites to cosmic and political explications. There are two reasons for this: religion is required as a foundation of belief and action on the part of the citizens; religion is required as an ultimate explanation of all laws and their preludes. The doctrine presented in the *Laws* would use religion, in the sense of rational theology, as an ultimate ontological explanation of what constitutes the political and moral "best." Hence in Book X of the *Laws* Plato presents rational arguments to prove: 1) that the gods exist; 2) that they care about human affairs; 3) that they cannot be won over by prayers and offerings.[42]

The prelude to all the preludes, then, is the set of religious propositions just stated which can be simply accepted as fact, or accepted after a reasoned argument has been given in support of

[40] 853b-d (tr. Bury).
[41] *Statesman* 301a (tr. J. B. Skemp).
[42] 888c ff.

them. The reasoned argument (*Laws* 887a-890d) presents the proofs for the three propositions and in addition a proof of the assertion that the soul is primary and that consequently all things related to soul, such as opinion, reflection, thought, art, and law are prior to matter.[43] Now the purpose in proving soul primary and matter secondary is to demonstrate that the motion which is self-moved is prior to that which is moved externally.[44] The self-moved souls which cause the heavenly bodies to move, and which are good, shall be called "gods." This is a demonstration by definition remarkably like that employed by Aquinas in his five proofs, for in both cases the demonstration concludes with the assertion, "and this I call god(s)." Plato argues:

> inasmuch as it has been shown that they [the heavenly bodies, months, seasons, years] are all caused by one or more souls, which are good also with all goodness, we shall declare these souls to be gods, whether it be that they order the whole heaven by residing in bodies, as living creatures, or whatever the mode and method.[45]

These souls, responsible for planetary and heavenly movement generally, are principles of motion which explain why matter is constantly in process of rearrangement. Not matter itself is the principle of motion, but soul which is primary and more basic than matter in the evolution of the cosmos.[46] But this is not the ultimate principle in the cosmos. Above these gods, or souls responsible for motion, there is a divine architect variously referred to by Plato as the demiurge, the king, the divine administrator and so on. He it is who orders the whole in accord with the highest good. The Athenian Stranger says:

> Let us persuade the young man by our discourse that all things are ordered systematically by Him who cares for the World-all with a view to the preservation and excellence of the Whole, whereof also each part, so far as it can, does and suffers what is proper to it. To each of these parts, down to the smallest fraction, rulers of their action and passion are appointed to bring about fulfilment even to

[43] 891e ff.
[44] 896 ff.
[45] *Laws* 899b (tr. Bury).
[46] For a discussion of Plato's explanations of motion, see J. B. Skemp, *The Theory of Motion in Plato's Later Dialogues* (Cambridge, England, 1942).

the uttermost fraction; whereof thy portion also, O perverse man, is one, and tends therefore always in its striving towards the All, tiny though it be. But thou failest to perceive that all partial generation is for the sake of the Whole, in order that for the life of the World-all blissful existence may be secured,—it not being generated for thy sake, but thou for its sake. . . . And inasmuch as soul, being conjoined now with one body, now with another, is always undergoing all kinds of changes either of itself or owing to another soul, there is left for the draughts-player no further task,—save only to shift the character that grows better to a superior place, and the worse to a worse, according to what best suits each of them, so that to each may be alloted its appropriate destiny.

Since our King saw that all actions involve soul, and contain much good and much evil, and that body and soul are, when generated, indestructible but not eternal, as are the gods ordained by law . . . and since He perceived that all soul that is good naturally tends always to benefit, but the bad to injure,—observing all this, He designed a location for each of the parts, wherein it might secure the victory of goodness in the Whole and the defeat of evil most completely, easily, and well. For this purpose He has designed the rule which prescribes what kind of character should be set to dwell in what kind of position and in what regions; but the causes of the generation of any special kind he left to the wills of each one of us men. For according to the trend of our desires and the nature of our souls, each one of us generally becomes of a corresponding character.[47]

Thus the divine architect of the cosmos must reckon with two principles over which he himself has no control: the principle of self-movement which Plato calls "soul" and the good of the Whole in accordance with which the order of things is determined. In like manner the statesman must organize the *polis* in terms of the characters of the men who make up the city (individual character being determined by the soul of a man), and in terms of the greatest good of the city, which is but one aspect of the good of the cosmos. Now just as the divine architect sees to it that each soul is appointed to its proper place in terms of the good or evil of its effects, so the statesman must see to it that within the city each man receives his proper place and position of power in terms of his moral stature.

[47] *Laws* 903b-904c (tr. Bury).

It is possible now to give at least a partial explication of the
analogy Plato wishes to make between the divine architect of the
cosmos and the statesman.[48] Both the divine craftsman or administrator and the statesman must exercise their knowledge and art
upon recalcitrant matter. For the cosmic artificer it is matter in
the universe at large which resists taking form and for the statesman it is human nature which is unruly and irrational, though
capable of being controlled by reason. Both therefore must fash-
ion an order (the whole of which constitutes the cosmos) in accordance with the demands of necessity, for necessity limits the
products of all craftsmen, divine and human.[49] The order they
establish, however, is structured in accordance with laws that determine the behavior of the parts (events or persons). If the structures, which are the work of reason as it occurs in the soul of the
divine craftsman and the statesman,[50] are the guiding principles
of the cosmos or state, then harmony and justice are achieved: if
not, chaos and evil result. The end or purpose of this order in
accordance with law is the Good which, as the most universal of
the ideas, exercises a directive influence upon reason. Thus the
end of the whole is excellence of existence, εὐδαίμων οὐσία, as stated
in the *Laws*,[51] whose perfect archetype is embodied in the Good.[52]
The whole cosmos, therefore, has an efficient, formal, material,
and final principle: the activity of reason and the art it employs is
the efficient principle; the ideas in the mind of the artisan are the
formal principle; the material to be worked with which, though
recalcitrant still is potentially formable to some degree, is the material principle; the realization of the Good is the final principle.
The proper adjustment and balancing of principles in the cosmos
and the state brings about a just order in which the virtues are ex-
emplified.

[48] The best studies of Plato's theology, and his theories of mind and soul
are Friedrich Solmsen, *Plato's Theology*, "Cornell Studies in Classical Philology," Vol. XXVII (Ithaca, 1942), and Harold Cherniss, *Aristotle's Criticism
of Plato and the Academy* (Baltimore, 1944), Vol. I, Appendix XI.
[49] Cf. *Laws* 818a-d.
[50] Cf. *Laws* 897b.
[51] *Laws* 903c.
[52] Cf. *Rep.* 508b-d; *Phaedrus* 247d; *Laws* 897b.

A religious ontology of the sort Plato argues as the prelude to his philosophy of law is far more elaborate and self-conscious than anything to be found in Aeschylus. But the *Oresteia* readily establishes the need for a philosophy of religion and politics. Plato, because of his philosophic interests, tried to answer the need, with what influence in his own city and in views that grew up three centuries later we know.[53] Any political organization, such as the Athenian city, that would weaken the force of ancestral religious beliefs and practices encourages its thoughtful citizens to the philosophical consideration of the place religion can and ought to have in the community. Plato's serious concern over the practicality of founding religion on political and philosophical requirements seems to be warranted because the optimistic assumption that Aeschylus makes, that a cosmic religion can replace a family religion, is not supported, at least in the outcome of events at Athens. Religion lost rather than gained political authority in the years after Aeschylus' death.

But of course the religious issue in the terms that Plato considers it is not a problem to be solved by Aeschylus; his concern as poet is to present the best action insofar as he can determine it. When his handling of the religious question is looked at from the point of view of dramatic requirements, it becomes clear that he is more concerned with the truth about the gods, simply represented, than about a philosophical justification of a set of beliefs. In other words, as the artist, Aeschylus is concerned to present an imitation of the action appropriate to the best men, and the beliefs about the gods which are true. From Plato's point of view Aeschylus' presentation would be politically salutary, for there the philosopher-statesman would find an imitation of the best action set over against an imitation of incontinent and unjust action. The *Oresteia* exhibits how men are moved by pleasure and and pain, rage and fear; it sets before the audience a hero whose

---

[53] See Rudolf Bultmann, *Primitive Christianity in Its Contemporary Setting* (New York, 1956), for a brief but penetrating discussion of the influence of Greek thought on early Christianity. Also, R. P. Winnington-Ingram, "A Religious Function of Greek Tragedy," *Journ. Hellen. Stud.*, LXXIV (1954), 16-24.

behavior is a model of piety and restraint even though driven by a god to commit a horrible act. It creates a world in which gods and men are given their proper places. Thus it appears that the artist, as one who makes or fashions something, must include the dramatist as well as the cosmic architect and the statesman. We may recall that passage in the *Laws* referred to above in which Plato explicitly compares the statesman to the tragedian.

In what respect is the dramatic artist to be compared with the architect of the universe and the statesman? Certainly Aeschylus regarded himself and was regarded by others (for example, Aristophanes in the *Frogs*) as a poet-statesman. But he does not legislate, he does not directly counsel the citizens of his state as the Law-wardens in Plato's *Laws* are expected to do.[54] Yet he does make available to them a spectacle which is primarily educative in function, and does this in accord with a set of moral principles (potential laws, as Plato suggests the content of drama ought to be) which determine the proper subject-matter and mode of action in the work of art. The best drama is one compatible with and beneficial to the laws of the city—in this case, it is a drama treating of piety, nobility in action, and the need for justice. But the dramatist of Aeschylus' stature accomplishes all this within the drama: that is, the drama is about the very thing which it itself lives up to. Aeschylus gives us the order that ought to obtain within the city by means of a drama which fits into that order. In that sense the poet is a real imitator, for he portrays the best order which the statesman and the world-creator themselves aim at. He sees it, as Plato would claim, as the work of others (of Athena and Zeus) for he is not himself the creator of that order. He, like the legislator, strives to give "representation of the fairest and best life." [55] The criterion for the best depends upon a distinction being made between truth and falsehood, noble and ignoble pleasure. It is within the drama itself that the distinction is drawn for the characters in their actions point out the different kinds of lives that men can lead. This portrayal of possibilities of conduct is in the hands of the poet; he is responsible for the action in the char-

[54] *Laws* XII.
[55] *Laws* 817b.

acters much as the gods are in the lives of men. And Aeschylus recognizes this parallel for he includes, in his imitation, the gods as divine influences and mediators.

The artist's relationship to his created characters is like that of the gods to men as Plato relates it:

> Let us suppose that each of us living creatures is an ingenious puppet of the gods, whether contrived by way of a toy of theirs or for some serious purpose—for as to that we know nothing; but this we do know, that these inward affections of ours, like sinews or cords, drag us along and, being opposed to each other, pull one against the other to opposite actions; and herein lies the dividing line between goodness and badness. For, as our argument declares, there is one of these pulling forces which every man should always follow and nowhere leave hold of, counteracting thereby the pull of the other sinews: it is the leading-string, golden and holy, of "calculation," entitled the public law of the State; and whereas the other cords are hard and steely and of every possible shape and semblance, this one is flexible and uniform, since it is of gold. With that most excellent leading-string of the law we must needs co-operate always; for since calculation is excellent, but gentle rather than forceful, its leading-string needs helpers to ensure that the golden kind within us may vanquish the other kinds.[56]

The public law of the state is the golden thread because it is of divine origin and in accord with divine intentions. It is the string with which men are led aright by their divine protectors. But it is not the only string. The "inward affections" which drag men this way and that are the pleasures and pains, desires and fears which are apt to overpower the golden thread.

The characters in Aeschylus' drama exhibit the same variety and conflict of motivations; only rarely does action follow the leading-string of noble conduct. But the conflict of good and evil and its consequences are made clear; the watching citizens will respond to what they see in terms of the effects the drama has on their motives and desires. The drama in its educative function will be supposed to influence the audience according to the various portrayals in the dramatic presentation. The dramatic artist

[56] *Laws* 644d-e.

is like a puppeteer in two senses: he controls the actions of his characters, and the behavior of the men who come to see his art.

Consequently the work of mind, such as a dramatic representation, can have this effect: it can exercise a control over the passions of those who witness it. One of the possible effects of a good imitation is then catharsis in some sense, i.e., a rechanneling of emotion or a striking of a new balance between the forces at work in the body. Both the poet and the legislator have this as their objective, for they are concerned to lead men to eschew the lower for the higher pleasures, the ignoble for the noble life.

In the *Oresteia* Athena and Orestes are representative of how this control of mind over passion can be brought about. They contrast with Clytemnestra, Aegisthus, and Agamemnon who fail in this respect. The effect on the audience ought to be to lead reflective individuals to emulate the better course of action. But the audience would necessarily be aware of the fact that to achieve the nobility of action which is represented by Orestes another agency is necessary: the help of Apollo who with his knowledge of purification can guide Orestes to and prepare him for his trial. The power of mind in the individual is not enough, especially when noble action depends upon the resolution of a moral problem, for laboring under the difficulty of determining what is right and what is wrong the individual may become confused and uncertain. Thus a purifying force must be introduced which will resolve doubt and enable men to follow the golden thread of godlike conduct. Apollo acts as this force within the drama; but the drama itself as an imitation of noble action can have this same effect upon the audience. What that purifying influence is and how it functions is our final concern.

CHAPTER FIVE

DRAMATIC AND MORAL MEANING
OF CATHARSIS

Nowhere is the high seriousness of the drama more evident than in the writing of Aeschylus; and nowhere has the place of art in the human community been more thoroughly examined than in the writing of the Greek philosophers Plato and Aristotle. From all that they have said, and from the great tragic tradition that they knew, it is evident that to the Athenian citizen the contribution of the artist to the city was of the greatest importance. Indeed, the tradition is an ancient one even for Athens, since the classical *polis* was preceded by a civilization that celebrated the achievements of art. Minoan Crete and Mycenaean Argos were profound influences on Athens, though often indirectly and by an unconscious affiliation that the Athenians themselves never ceased to wonder about. Homer, their historian of that world, speaks to them of a time when men lived in feudal communities under the rule of a king. Agamemnon was just such a king who ruled in fabled Argos or Mycenae. That world was one in which the achievements of art were rich; the Minoan-Mycenaean world is in its mode of life and physical organization aesthetic. There is, in the remains we have recently come to know, evidence of an artistic impulse so inventive and so stylistically creative that the later geometric and classical styles appear restrained in comparison. Yet the aestheticism of the Minoan-Mycenaean civilization is a reason for suspecting that the literary and philosophical achievements of Hellenic Athens would be impossible for the earlier age. Whether or not there was a literary tradition in Crete and in the Peloponnesus beyond the retelling of myths many of which passed into the classical world we may never know. But one suspects that the society which produced Minos, Agamemnon, and Nestor would not be able to produce a Homer, far less an inquirer into nature. The remains of Crete and Mycenae suggest that in imitating the incredible splendors of nature the society hoped to propitiate the natural powers it feared.[1]

The change that comes about in the sixth and fifth centuries is the more remarkable because of its philosophic temperament. A city that maintains drama festivals is far removed from one that sponsors rodeos. While in Knossos art was used as a manifestation of grandeur and an instrument of control, in Athens art became a way of celebrating the human and the divine, of stating the truth, and of instructing men. What remains of the Minoan-Mycenaean past is a lesson for the Athenian present. Aeschylus uses that past in his recreation of the present, and enables his audience to see a continuity.

The artist composes a world out of memory and desire, shapes it according to need and necessity, animates it with the metabolic, the inspirational, and the daimonic. From cosmic necessity and human caprice he brings a new order of possibility to the world and ineluctability to action. Where nature was obdurate and man impotent, after the transformation of art nature's imaginative pliability is joined to human purpose. Where once experience was suffered, it now conserves and creates. Where the divine beset the human, the human now explains the divine. Thus the mimetic works a transformation which, in art as in philosophy, discloses a fundamental compatibility in what is seemingly dissonant.

The artist is fundamentally a maker, and like all makers is bridled by the limits of necessity and probability. The boundaries of necessity and probability are determined by the nature of the material and the goal of making: like the cosmic creator and the statesman, the artist bends his organization to a definite purpose. Insofar as a writer like Aeschylus goes to the traditional stories for his dramatic subject he is conscious of producing an imitation, but this artistic activity is not controlled exclusively by what we would call an aesthetic end. Rather, it is controlled by the aesthetic only as that is in turn controlled by the political,

[1] The best photographic presentation of the Minoan-Mycenaean sites and remains is Spyridon Marinatos' *Kreta und das mykenische Hellas* (Munich, 1959). Speculation on the continuity of the Minoan-Mycenaean and the classical world is interestingly entertained by T. B. L. Webster, *From Mycenae to Homer* (London, 1958).

i.e., the moral and intellectual needs, as well as the sensuous grati-
fications, of men living together. Aeschylus' plays are intended
for an audience of fellow citizens who share a common past and
aspire to a common political good. The artist has his place in that
community because of a specific contribution he can make as an
artist: he realizes his obligation insofar as he produces what is
best in the drama.

In realizing what is best the artist, like the statesman and the
cosmic creator, must wrestle with an intractable material. This
intractability is due to the disparity that necessarily exists between
the ideal order known by reason and the realization of that order
in a material. This can only be overcome through knowledge, per-
fected techniques, and a divine gift. To the Hellenic intellect
there were significant analogies to be drawn between the making
of worlds, of states, and of dramas. A schematic presentation of
the analogies is to be found in the Appendix, page 145.

From an examination of the *Oresteia* in the light of classical
philosophical speculation on art, we can see more clearly how
this kind of drama was expected to contribute to the life of the
polis and how its value was determined in the face of competitive
claim from religion and philosophy.

All making, since it presupposes the work of an intelligent being, is essentially a separating out of relevant and irrelevant elements. Thus the artist seeks to discover and order what is best,
most efficacious, and proper in his work, and at the same time to
exclude what is irrational. In the case of the tragic dramatist, this
is first performed in the structuring of the plot. As the *Poetics*
makes clear, the plot is by far the most important part of the
drama; it is, in fact, the "initiating principle" (ἀρχή) and "soul"
(ψυχή) of the work.[2] Therefore it is in the structuring of the plot
that the poet must exercise all his skill and knowledge, for only
if the plot is well made will the tragedy achieve its proper goal,
the presentation of an adequate aesthetic object which produces

---

[2] "The plot is the first essential and the soul of tragedy; character comes
second. . . . It is the action which is the object of imitation; the individual
characters are subsidiary to it" (*Poetics,* tr. G. M. A. Grube [New York, 1958],
6. 1450a39-1450b5).

its own proper pleasure in the beholder. The excellence which, according to Aristotle, tragedy ought to have is well stated in the twenty-sixth chapter of the *Poetics* where tragedy is compared to the epic:

> tragedy contains all the elements of the epic—it can even use epic meter—and besides these, it has the important elements of music which stirs us to pleasures most vividly, and of spectacle. Indeed, it has vividness both in the reading and the performance. And it fulfills the purpose of its imitation in a smaller compass. The more compact is more pleasing than that which is spread over a great length of time. . . .
>
> If, then, tragedy excels in all these ways and also in its artistic function, for no art must arouse just any kind of pleasure but only that which is appropriate to it, then tragedy achieves its purpose better and is superior to the epic.[3]

Economy and effectiveness are to be achieved by selecting an action of a certain kind, presenting it with order and proper magnitude, choosing a protagonist (hero) of a certain kind (this is in part done for the poet because he most likely will, indeed ought to, rely on familiar stories of some antiquity), ordering the language by means of stylistic elegance, and embellishing the representation by music and appropriate spectacle. In short, the largest part of the *Poetics* is devoted to laying down the directives for coming closest to the mark in matters of tragic mimesis.

Aristotle's exhortation is to know the end of tragedy, as a kind of literature with its proper pleasure, and to remove from the artistic product all that would detract from that end. The pleasure of tragedy is one which comes from the representation of fearful and pitiable events. These have been carefully chosen and purged of any irrelevant material, for this is the effect of the making process in which the artist is engaged. When these events are presented to an audience they produce a response and an attendant pleasure which is itself purged of all excesses and irrelevancies. Thus the dramatist structures his work of art by means of a process of selection, of separating out, in order that an emotional

[3] *Poetics* 26. 1462a13-1462b15 (tr. Grube).

and intellectual separating out may be achieved in the beholder. The problem that concerns us in making clear the import of the *Oresteia* for the concept of catharsis is to determine the nature of the dramatic structuring, and the psychological process which makes the desired outcome possible.

The *Oresteia* is concerned with "purification" both ritualistically and dramatically; it is a drama of human action beginning in crime and moral confusion, and ending in reconciliation and moral enlightenment. Further, if we accept Aeschylus seriously as the poet who knows what is right for the *polis*, his drama ought to have an effect on the audience which is one of enlightenment.

If we think about the *Oresteia* in this way we will, I believe, come to understand what the special problems of the poet are insofar as he is taken to be the rival of the statesman in matters of pedagogy and rule. Further, we will see that the concept of catharsis is indeed connotatively rich enough to be of great value to the philosopher and literary critic, for the concept has a political, moral, and religious aspect, as well as a definite aesthetic application. This serviceability will explain its widespread employment, and will show the absurdity of trying to relate catharsis to one specific usage, medical, religious, or horticultural, as has often been attempted in the past.

A great variety of interpretations of catharsis have been offered as part of the astoundingly rich accumulation of commentaries on the *Poetics*,[4] but it is not until the Renaissance that Aristotle's use of catharsis is brought up for serious investigation. The variety of interpretations developed then seemed to satisfy later critics who accepted one or the other of them, so that the disputes

---

[4] The best bibliographical sources on the *Poetics* in general and catharsis in particular are the following: L. Cooper and A. Gudeman, "A Bibliography of the *Poetics* of Aristotle," *Cornell Studies in English*, XI (1928); M. T. Herrick, "A Supplement to Cooper and Gudeman's Bibliography of the *Poetics* of Aristotle," *American Journal of Philology*, LII (1931), 168-74; S. H. Butcher, *Aristotle's Theory of Poetry and Fine Art* (New York, 1951); G. F. Else, "A Survey of Works on Aristotle's *Poetics*," *Classical Weekly*, XLVIII, No. 6 (1955); Hellmut Flashar, "Die medizinischen Grundlagen der Lehre von der Wirkung der Dichtung in der griechischen Poetik," *Hermes*, LXXXIV (1956), 12-48.

about catharsis in drama become familiar and repetitive.[5] Then in the nineteenth century the discussion assumed new vigor with the publication of Bernays' thesis that catharsis could be explained in terms of a medical analogy,[6] and in the early years of this century with the contention on the part of the Cambridge classicists that catharsis could be interpreted in terms of ritual.[7] In the past fifty years several new attempts have been made to interpret the meaning of catharsis in the *Poetics* and elsewhere by analyzing the contexts in which the term appears and then explicating it as a member of a family of related concepts. To accomplish this task it has been necessary to examine all the uses of catharsis, and to consider the philosophical motivation for the usage, rather than, as had often been the case in the past, merely the philological motivation. Thus the dialogues of Plato and the entire corpus of Aristotelian writings have been searched for clues, with the result of establishing, on a much more solid base than heretofore, a pattern of philosophical ideas among which catharsis takes its place. There is no intention here of re-examining all these views since this has been done by several writers, nor in entering into the details of disputes over interpretations. It will concern us, however, to state the main varieties of interpretation, to see what aspect of the total aesthetic situation each one

[5] For a summary of the Renaissance views, see the article "Catharsis" by Baxter Hathaway in *Dictionary of World Literature*, ed. Joseph T. Shipley (New York, 1943). Some of these positions are discussed by Thomas Twining in his commentary on the *Poetics*, still one of the best. Twining accepted the view, maintained by Minturno and Milton, that the pity and fear aroused in the spectator by the drama drive out the like emotions which are native to men, especially those of melancholic temperament: a variant of the homeopathic interpretation. (*Aristotle's Treatise on Poetry*, London, 1789.) For a brief historical survey of definitions of tragedy down to the seventeenth century, see A. Philip McMahon, "Seven Questions on Aristotelian Definitions of Tragedy and Comedy," *Harvard Studies in Classical Philology*, XL (1929), 97-198.

[6] Jacob Bernays, *Grundzüge der verlorenen Abhandlung des Aristoteles über die Wirkung der Tragödie* (Breslau, 1857), and *Zwei Abhandlungen über die Aristotelische Theorie des Dramas* (Berlin, 1880).

[7] Cf. Jane Harrison, *Themis* and *Prolegomena to the Study of Greek Religion*.

has selected for emphasis, and then, by means of both aesthetic and psychological principles which have emerged in the foregoing chapters, to suggest what seems to be a plausible reconstruction of the concept of catharsis as it is used in the analysis of tragic drama. Each of the main types of interpretation seizes upon some important aspect of the total aesthetic situation but fails to consider to what degree that one aspect, if developed in isolation, meets the demands of an adequate philosophy of Greek drama. It is my belief that this can more readily be realized if the *Oresteia* in particular is considered, because it embodies dramatic and philosophical elements essential to an understanding of Greek dramatic theory. But in addition we must read the Athenian philosophers and playwrights with our own experience of tragic drama in mind.

The interpretations of catharsis are of four kinds. The first considers catharsis to refer to a therapeutic process in which excessive and harmful emotions are eliminated in order that the soul can resume its proper balance. This interpretation grows out of the emphasis in both Plato and Aristotle upon the emotions as deleterious superfluities which result from some imbalance of physical humors or psychological states. This belief, in itself a common one among Greek thinkers, has its roots in Pythagorean and Hippocratic views of the human organism as compounded of various elements which must maintain a harmony if the individual is to function well. Excess or deficiency of one element produces general malaise; reconstitution of the proper proportion of elements restores physical and psychological health. Excess of one element or humor is dealt with by a "purging" or a "separating out" for which process the term "catharsis" is used. By analogy, the temperamental elements of the soul could be seen as requiring like treatment.

This common usage in the Pythagorean and Hippocratic writings, as well as the Platonic and Aristotelian, led Bernays and Weil to suggest that the catharsis of the emotions which tragic drama supposedly produces is to be understood by analogy with the medical practices of the day. Pent up emotions are spent in the experience of witnessing the dramatic spectacle; the result is a soothed, calmed soul and a beholder psychologically "tranquilized."

Such an interpretation has its proponents in recent writing as well as in that of the last century.[8] The posthumous lectures of Humphrey House [9] are careful to point out the danger of staying too close to the medical implications of catharsis (something House dislikes in the interpretations of his predecessors, I. Bywater and S. H. Butcher), but he nevertheless maintains that catharsis refers to the relief from "overcharged emotions." He seeks to connect the dramatic use of catharsis with Aristotle's moral theory:

> A tragedy rouses the emotions from potentiality to activity by worthy and adequate stimuli; it controls them by directing them to the right objects in the right way; and exercises them, within the limits of the play, as the emotions of the good man would be exercised. When they subside to potentiality again after the play is over, it is a more "trained" potentiality than before. This is what Aristotle calls κάθαρσις. Our responses are brought nearer to those of the good and wise man. . . . The result of the catharsis is an emotional balance and equilibrium: and it may well be called a state of emotional health.[10]

In doing so he moves closer to the second view, that catharsis refers to a universalizing of emotions, but does not quite articulate it since he believed that the actual "exercising" of the emotions was essential in achieving a kind of internal harmony, and that the medical connotation is significant.

This first interpretation can also embody some elements of the fourth, that catharsis refers to a redemptive process, for when the medical emphasis is explored metaphorically, as it was by the Greeks themselves, the purgation effected is ceremonial, i.e., a

---

[8] The recent expressions of this view, following Bernays in the main, are: F. L. Lucas, *Tragedy* (London, 1928). Lucas thinks the view is wrong, but believes Aristotle maintained it. Max Kommerell, *Lessing und Aristoteles* (Frankfurt-am-Main, 1940). Margaret J. Myers, "The Meaning of Katharsis," *Sewanee Review*, XXXIV (1926), 278-90. F. Dirlmeier, "Katharsis Pathematon," *Hermes*, LXXV (1940), 81-92.

[9] *Aristotle's Poetics* (London, 1956).

[10] *Ibid.*, pp. 109-10.

kind of religious lustration. Thus it is but a step from the belief that physical purging produces harmony in the organism to the belief that the cleansing of the unclean initiate makes him pure so that he can participate in the celebration of the mysteries.

The interpretation of catharsis as a medical concept assumes that the purging of excessive emotions is effected by a conflict of powers: the congenital passions of pity and fear are opposed by an external source of like but stronger emotions. In the ensuing conflict, the congenital emotions are driven out. This view then must go on to maintain either that the new source of emotion replaces the old (at best this could be but a momentary exchange) or that the new emotions, which have been induced, are then tranquilized and subdued by the conclusion of the drama. But on this point the various writers are vague.

What does emerge on this interpretation is the assumption that tragic drama exists as a means to a psycho-social end. The fact that the drama can effect a purgation means that it is an important instrument for the control and organization of individuals in large groups, as well as an effective medication. There is no doubt but that in Aristotle's mind the actual emotional effect is a strong one, a purifying one, and in general a superior one to the like effect of the enthusiasm engendered by the celebration of the mysteries. But it is doubtful whether a philosopher with his sense of the special qualities and purposes of every kind of thing would have limited his meaning of catharsis to such factors in his analysis of the tragic drama. If he did mean it in such a narrow sense, it is clearly inadequate. The emphasis in this first view falls on the psychological condition of the beholder and upon an effect which tragic drama perhaps has, but an effect which tells us little about its essential characteristics and excellences. Assuming Aristotle held the view, it leaves unexplained the positive moral consequences of having the cathartic experience.

The second interpretation considers catharsis as a knowing, intellectual, or quasi-cognitive process, in the sense that the result of the "separating out" is the universalizing of pity and fear. This view maintains that the *emotions* themselves are purified, which generally is taken to mean purged of their egocentric reference.

Catharsis refers to the separating out of the bad elements in these emotional states from the better ones, the latter then rendered measured and harmonious, thus assisting the beholder to deeper religious and moral insight. When this occurs the emotions, once painful and frightening, are themselves aesthetically satisfying.

This view is developed, in part on philological grounds, by L. A. Post [11] who points out that the word "catharsis" is not limited, like the English word "purgation," to the elimination of impurities, but rather includes all processes of separating one part from another part, as in our words "refining," "purifying," "pressing," "clearing of the mind," "expressing," "skimming off," etc. Consequently, "Tragic catharsis does not get rid of emotion or of excess emotion, nor does it merely refine emotion. It rids the mind of emotional confusion or lack of control by making the emotion objective, by separating it from the rational mind, which is the self. The thinker is aware of his emotion without identifying himself with it." [12] Post sees a usage similar to Aristotle's, as he construes it, in the *Sophist* and the *Timaeus* of Plato:

> There are some striking passages in Plato that explain with great probability what Aristotle had in mind. In the pseudo-Platonic *Definitions* catharsis is defined as the separation of better from worse. This probably derives from a passage in Plato's *Sophist* in which examples are given such as sifting or winnowing. The means by which separation is effected in such cases is agitation. In the *Timaeus* Plato holds that fire, earth, air, and water in the physical universe are separated by pressure as liquid is separated from solid in the extraction of juice from grapes or oil from olives.[13]

Now, when this is applied to the emotional reaction of the audience witnessing a tragedy, the conclusion is drawn that "catharsis" in its dramatic meaning refers to the universalizing of emotion, for only in that way could it be reasonable, and not merely a form of psychological agitation.

This interpretation is pushed further, with less concern for phi-

---

[11] *From Homer to Menander*, "Sather Classical Lectures," Vol. XXIII (Berkeley, 1951).

[12] *Ibid.*, p. 321; footnote, p. 320.

[13] *Ibid.*, pp. 263-64.

lology, by E. P. Papanoutsos [14] who stresses the reasonableness of
the emotional state which results, and the harmony that obtains
between the purified emotions and the intelligibility of the universe. He rejects the interpretations of catharsis which claim that
it is a process of removing or neutralizing the emotions of pity
and fear:

> Le but qu'il [Aristotle] poursuivait étant de défendre la poésie
> tragique, sur le plan moral, il ne pouvait pas dire que sa tâche
> consistait à épurer l'âme de la pitié et de la crainte ou à la rendre
> moins sensible et moins encline à éprouver ces émotions, mais, au
> contraire, à épurer ces passions pour en faire des dispositions et des
> tendances compatibles avec le "χρηστὸν ἦθος." [15]

In their place he suggests the following:

> La poésie tragique, qui a pour tâche d'émouvoir la crainte et la
> pitié et d'associer à elles le sentiment moral et religieux d'humanité,
> épure ce genre de passions, et par conséquent amène l'âme à goûter
> non pas la crainte et la pitié ordinaires, c'est à dire des emotions
> dénuées de toute signification particulière, des sentiments déraison-
> nables et indisciplinés, ordinairement en désaccord entre eux, et
> dont l' "amétrie" rompt l'harmonie intérieure de l'âme, mais une
> crainte et une pitié épurées, c'est à dire des émotions qui jaillissent
> dans notre âme au moment où nous saissons un sens moral et re-
> ligieux profond, et du fait que nous avons saisi ce sens. Il s'agit,
> comme on le voit, d'émotions d'une autre *qualité,* de passions
> "raisonnables" et "mesurées," en harmonie entre elles et avec l'en-
> semble de l'universe psychique, qui non seulement n'affaiblissent pas
> la résistance de la raison aux impulsions des instincts, mais encore
> font accéder l'homme à une sphère morale et religieuse supérieure.
> La joie plus profonde qu'il en éprouve se concilie ainsi avec l'éthos
> vertueux, et a de droit, sa place dans la vie de l'esprit.[16]

[14] *La catharsis des passions d'après Aristote* (Athens, 1953).

[15] *Ibid.,* pp. 29-30. "The end which he [Aristotle] sought being to defend
tragic poetry on a moral basis, he could not say that its task consisted in purifying the soul of pity and fear, or in making it less sensitive and less inclined
to experience those emotions; but on the contrary, to purify those emotions
and to transform them into inclinations and tendencies compatible with the
'χρηστὸν ἦθος' [good character]."

[16] *Ibid.,* pp. 26-27. "Tragic poetry, which aims at arousing fear and pity
and connecting them with the moral and religious feeling of humaneness,
purges those passions, and consequently leads the soul to feel not ordinary

Similar views to those of Post and Papanoutsos are maintained by classical scholars in various traditions.[17] Although the specific details of interpretation differ, this way of dealing with catharsis seems to grow out of a belief that the spectator at the dramatic presentation sees in the suffering of the hero something universal, applicable to all men, and that this "vision" arouses something more than mere pity and fear, something close to a revelation of the moral condition of mankind. The effect of this insight is to remove the individual from the restrictions of pity and fear, which are either congenital or aroused empathetically by observing the action, to the apprehension of the *nature* of pity and fear. This is made possible, if the drama is a good one, by the paradigmatic nature of the action and the hero's suffering. Thus this experience in reality subdues the passions (both those the spectator came with and those aroused in the theater) and releases the rational powers of the soul which are enabled, by the agency of the plot, to behold the nature of man, of human destiny and suffering. The outcome, then, is a new and deeper knowledge. Hence I have maintained that this makes of catharsis a knowing or cognitive process.

This position is attractive because it makes the aesthetic experience one of moral insight, and thus accords with the general intellectual concerns of both Plato and Aristotle. It has the further advantage of allowing one to say that ideally at least the tragic

---

pity and fear—that is, emotion stripped of all specific meaning, of irrational and undisciplined sentiments, usually inharmonious among themselves, and whose lack of measure breaks the inner harmony of the soul—but a refined fear and a refined pity, i.e., emotions which burst forth from our soul when we comprehend a profound moral and religious meaning, and have truly grasped that meaning. It is a question, one realizes, of emotions of another quality, of 'reasonable' and 'proportioned' passions, in harmony among themselves and with the whole of the psychic universe. They not only do not weaken the opposition of reason to the forces of instinct, but allow man to approach a higher moral and religious sphere. The profounder joy which man feels through this experience reconciles it with the moral ideal of virtue, and thus it has, by rights, its proper place in the life of the spirit."

[17] For example, see Louis Moulinier, *Le pur et l'impur dans la pensée des Grecs; d'Homère à Aristote* (Paris, 1952), especially p. 419. K. Volkmann-Schluck, "Die Lehre von der Katharsis in der *Poetik* des Aristoteles," *Varia Variorum* (1952), 104-17.

drama could reveal truths about the human condition and the self. Since the purification is of the emotions without removing them, it can be said that Aristotle meant pity and fear to be important (one must experience those emotions) and at the same time meant them to be something revelatory of their own genesis and meaning.

It is clear that the exercise of reason is not going to be the result of witnessing tragic drama in all cases, not even when the drama is a good one, and that the moral insight and religious experience engendered by the drama is not an intellectual experience for the majority of theatergoers. It is doubtful whether even Plato and Aristotle would think it ought to be that kind of experience; given the facts of the human and political order, few men are equipped to suffer catharsis of the kind just described. And yet for all men the aesthetic experience can rightly be said to be one in which the direct impact of self-regarding emotions is lessened and the affective condition "tied" to something other than the self. It is quite correct to see in catharsis a moral element; but it is necessary to supplement that with a political and psychological element, as we shall see.

The suggestion that catharsis refers to an artistic or aesthetic process has been developed, as far as I know, by only one commentator in recent years, G. F. Else. In his book, *Aristotle's Poetics: The Argument* (Cambridge, England, 1957), he modifies his earlier stand which, he now believes, put too much stress on the purely artistic aspects of the drama.[18] However, the aesthetic interpretation of catharsis is of interest because it brings the *Poetics* in line with recent literary criticism which on the whole has tended to favor an aesthetic interpretation at the risk of slighting the psychological and moral dimensions of art. When Else sets forth his earlier position he argues that the catharsis of the emotions is meaningful only if we interpret it as implying that the spectators' pleasure is purified as a direct consequence of a properly constructed plot. He sees Aristotle as elaborating and refining

[18] Else, "Aristotle on the Beauty of Tragedy," *Harv. Stud. Class. Philol.*, XLIX (1938), 179-204. For Else's modifications, see his book, especially pp. 436-50.

certain views of Plato on pleasure and art. While the latter maintained that pleasure could be purified, he did not see the possibility of a pure pleasure resulting from the witnessing of tragic drama. To this Aristotle replies that the drama can be the source of a pure pleasure *if the drama is properly made*. Else goes on to say:

> The true pleasure given by a tragedy or an epic poem, then, flows from its perfection of form as surely as the pleasure given by a statue or a painting or a melody.
>
> Tragedy, then, strives to attain a symmetry or due proportion of the passions. This is not an ethical concept; and it does not mean simply that pity and fear are reduced to moderation, but that they are impregnated with the measure and beauty of the drama as a whole.
>
> The crux of the matter is that the poetic catharsis is primarily an artistic rather than a psychological process. It takes place essentially in the tragedy when it is composed, not in the soul of the spectator when he sees it performed. This does not mean that it has nothing to do with the spectator; but it does mean that it has nothing to do with a cure or treatment of him. . . . The making of a tragedy implies a spectator, as a statue is made to be seen and a piece of music to be heard. But it does not necessarily imply the individual member of the audience, with all his idiosyncrasies and imperfections. In the *Poetics* the spectator is present not as a man but as an ideal destination, a fixed point of reference toward which the work is aimed; it is assumed implicitly that when it reaches this point the psychological effect will follow as a matter of course. Not, perhaps, for groundlings; but Aristotle did not shape his theory for them.
>
> This ideal spectator is not the παθητικός described in the *Politics*, who needs relief from his passions; and it is not the true function of tragedy to give such relief. Pity and fear are not first set loose in all their painful reality, to prey on the spectator's soul, and then somehow exorcised; they are purified in the same moment that they are aroused, by their incorporation into the beauty and measure of the perfect whole. In this purified state they are the basis—the indispensable basis—of the pure pleasure which a great tragedy calls forth in the soul.[19]

Else's position shifts the emphasis from the beholder to the structure of the drama; the locus of catharsis is now seen to be in

[19] *Ibid.*, pp. 195, 198, 199-201.

the work itself, rather than in the audience, as the first two positions maintained. Of course the response of the audience is involved, for the pure pleasure appropriate to the tragic drama is experienced only if the plot is itself "purged" of those elements which are emotionally disturbing (i.e., the accidental, the barbaric, the capricious, the implausible). The pleasure which the drama affords is the result of its possessing harmony, due measure, limit: πέρας and συμμετρία.[20] And because it has these characteristics it stimulates only emotions (a more neutral word such as "responses" is perhaps more appropriate here) which are pure and ordered. Therefore this position objects to the first one, namely, that catharsis refers to a homeopathic cure for the spectator. This, Else maintained, is to confuse the aesthetic and the psychological aspects of the total dramatic situation. In recognizing this confusion, the third interpretation of catharsis rightly calls attention to the importance of the aesthetic. Yet, as Else himself maintains in amending this view, there is an emotional side to tragic pleasure which is here overlooked. Pity and fear must be present, but "authorized and released by an intellectually conditioned structure of action. The emotion flows unimpeded *because* when we feel it we feel it as justified and inevitable." [21]

The position which concerns us finally is the one which maintains that catharsis is a redemptive process. This might be considered an elaboration of the first view, that catharsis refers to a kind of homeopathic cure, but deserves separate consideration because it prefers the religious connotation of the term to the medical. Usually the position is presented in terms of the purification of the hero, through his suffering and increased understanding. Like the gods celebrated in the mystery rituals, the hero falls to be redeemed; and the spectator feels himself "purged," i.e., redeemed or saved because he participates in the action of the hero or god. Thus the consequence or catharsis in this sense is the restoration of some positive relationship between the individual and the supernatural.

This position is backed up by two kinds of evidence: 1) that

[20] *Ibid.*, pp. 183-85.
[21] *Aristotle's Poetics: The Argument*, p. 449.

from anthropological studies which see the origin of tragedy in the mystery religions which preceded the art; 2) that from an examination of man's longing for god, the need to establish spiritual contact with some "other" in the cosmos.

The anthropological version of this interpretation makes much of the fact that tragedy is closely associated with religious and mythical beliefs; that it undoubtedly did develop from religious celebrations, and that it has a strong element of the supernatural in it. But it is doubtful whether Aristotle or we would find the parallel between the fallen and redeemed vegetation god and the tragic hero sufficient to account for the effect of drama. In fact, there is good evidence that Aristotle set the drama and the rituals of the religious celebrants over against each other. He saw some common properties which they possessed, but insisted that the effect of the drama was different both in its means and ends from religious enthusiasm.

The more directly religious emphasis, which argues that the effect of drama is to re-establish some relationship between men and the supernatural "other" in the cosmos, is more difficult to deal with, for it claims that the experience of the spectator is a special one, to be likened only to a specific religious experience. In brief, this is the awareness on the part of all men that there is something strange, divine, "wholly other" in the universe. The awareness arouses emotions of pity and fear, which are further exacerbated by the "seeing" of manifestations of this otherness, as in the fate of a tragic hero. But these emotions are removed in the aesthetic experience of the drama by seeing as well the redemption or salvation of the hero. Pity and fear are thereby translated into the emotion of awe, and awe into reverence.[22] The salvation of the hero is effected by his action, and his stature is increased through his suffering.

The audience recognizes the possibility for redemption in this paradigmatic action; and is led therefore to reaffirm its faith in the supernatural agencies responsible for this outcome, and to seek reunion with the supernatural.

[22] This view is elaborated by Philip Wheelwright, *The Burning Fountain*.

This view assumes that tragedy is essentially religious in its theme and function, if by religious one means assertion of existence of the divine and the means whereby this can be affirmed for the individual. The hero, it is assumed, is one who "falls" and is "saved"; he is one "purified" in such a way that the audience is "purified" too.

This view, like the previous one, tends to place the locus of catharsis in the drama, but now with the emphasis on the experience of the tragic hero, rather than on the plot. It suffers from a kind of psychological overspecialization, even though it claims that the attitudes and sequence of affective states it selects for consideration are common to men. They may be, but the drama is not necessarily the agency of eliciting such experience. However, there is no question but that the hero is one who in some sense or other is "redeemed" in that he is not one hated, reviled, or often even blamed; truly he has gained insight into himself, and the audience with him. But that does not necessarily mean that the audience is convinced of and attracted to a supernatural force in the cosmos as requiring addressive response. This view, like the three others, says something significant about the nature of the tragic drama, but like the others it is but part of the total aesthetic situation. While each of these positions preserves something of the complex transaction which provides the conditions for tragic drama, and while each one can be buttressed by passages from the writings of Plato and Aristotle, it is clear that no one of them satisfactorily explains the dramatic situation and offers an acceptable interpretation of catharsis. Which one is closest to Aristotle's original meaning it is impossible to say. The remarkable fact is that his writings are rich enough to provide evidence for each of these positions, though they do not contain sufficient elaboration to make any one of them the most likely.

They serve us well by directing our attention to certain aspects of the dramatic situation that we can appreciate as significant. But all of them, it seems to me, are too little concerned with the dramatic situation as a whole. Before we consider that here, it will be helpful to add to the four interpretations of catharsis subjects which both Plato and Aristotle considered essential to an explication of catharsis and to the behavior of human beings in emotionally charged situations.

From the earliest remains of Greek philosophical writing it is readily seen that there was an abiding concern to understand the behavior and claims of men possessed by strong emotions. During the period of philosophical flowering in the fourth century, that concern was still a central one and both Plato and Aristotle carry further the investigations begun by their Ionian predecessors. Why the phenomena, which for convenience can be grouped under the heading "enthusiasm," were of such interest is not known with any certainty, but some conjectures can be made about it. The development of medicine as a science; the fact of "inspiration" widely observed in the poet, the prophet, the religious celebrant; the inquiry into the powers of human reason; the contradictory claims made by philosophers and those who said they were possessed by the gods: all of these circumstances occurring in the society that we know as Greek undoubtedly led to the repeated attempt to understand emotional problems.

Several recent studies have discussed the interest, both theoretical and practical, which Greek writers had in "irrational" phenomena.[23] Previous chapters here have shown that one of the main themes in the *Oresteia* is the irrational frenzy of a morality of revenge as contrasted with the rational deliberation of a legalistic morality. Further, it was suggested that Aeschylus, like Plato and Aristotle, was concerned to examine the nature of fear, its place and means for its control in the *polis*. The drama as a social institution is regarded by all three as dealing with the irrational and the rational sides of man, for all three see in the drama a representation of types of human conduct and temperament which in their structuring produce a wide range of response in the beholder. And finally, all three are concerned to know what the political and moral consequences of the total dramatic situation may be.

[23] The most recent is E. R. Dodds, *The Greeks and the Irrational* (Berkeley, 1951). Two earlier studies are of importance, J. Croissant, *Aristote et les mystères,* "Bibliothèque de la faculté de philosophie et lettres de l'université de Liège," No. 51 (1942), and A. Delatte, *Les conceptions de l'enthousiasme chez les philosophes présocratique* (Paris, 1934).

The problem that seems to lie behind the introduction of the concept of catharsis arises when one asks if knowledge and the means of attaining it, if self-control and the means of achieving it, are compatible with the experience that the tragic drama and related forms of activity provide. This problem must be solved if one is to know who can legitimately claim to have knowledge and who can properly teach political virtue. Aeschylus, it can be inferred from the few dramas of his left to us, shared this concern, although his inquiry is not conducted in philosophical terms, but rather exhibited in the content of his writing. From the *Oresteia* in particular it is evident that he took the role of the artist as knower and teacher seriously; it is in the context of this concern with knowing and teaching that the concept of catharsis can be most useful. To appreciate, therefore, the significance of this concept to those thinkers who first elaborated it, we need to ask whether or not a man who is inspired by a kind of enthusiasm and in turn produces a kind of enthusiasm in those he addresses can ever be a true knower and teacher.

This very question is put to us, I believe, by the action of the *Oresteia* when Apollo, the god of prophecy, dreams, and art, directs and subsequently defends Orestes. Does he speak the truth? Or is he possessed by a kind of madness like that he inspires in his own priestess? There is something bizarre in his testimony when compared with the firm deliberations of Athena. Yet he does speak the truth.

Among men the truthfulness of the enthusiast, one who is in the grip of a strong passion presumably inspired by a god, is difficult to evaluate. And the poet was generally regarded as one who spoke while possessed. Plato presents the poet as one through whom the muse speaks; but the muse does not guarantee the truthfulness of the utterances, and certainly the poet himself cannot be held responsible, for he claims to be but the instrument of an external power. He quite literally does not know what he is talking about.[24]

Yet what he asserts might be true; and there are philosophical utterances that come to the gifted man in similar ways which are

24 Cf. *Meno* 99c, *Timaeus* 72a, *Laws* 801b.

true. It is worth recalling in this connection that in the opening of the *Symposium* Socrates is said to have stopped on his way to the party, lost in thought, and similar "seizures" of his are mentioned later on. This kind of philosophic ecstacy is contrasted with the ecstatic states of the artist later on in the conversation. Plato wished to assert that there were reliable and unreliable daimonomanias.[25]

Plato solves this problem through the distinction he makes between good and bad imitation, between the copying of mere appearances, and the knowing of eternal orders which can guide the making of the true artist.[26] All human making is a process of imitation as far as Plato is concerned, and the varieties of imitation can only be evaluated in terms of the model and the skill of the artisan. But the true enthusiast claims to have more than a vision; he is one possessed by a god, and he asserts the truth of his prophecy or poem on the basis of supernatural infallibility. On this point Plato, like Aristotle, sees no evidence of supernatural influences. He regards the agitation of the enthusiast as a manifestation of passion, the result of an imbalance in the soul and a kind of delirium.[27] Plato does not doubt that the induced agitation has a curative effect upon the enthusiast: eventually a psychological and physical tranquility imposes itself. But the explanation that he gives is thoroughly naturalistic, based on physiological and psychological principles. He rejects any explanation that would assign the cure to a god.

The same is true of Aristotle who sees enthusiasm as the consequence of a melancholy character.[28] The ecstasy of the enthusiast

[25] Cf. J. Tate, "Plato and Didacticism," *Hermathena*, XLVIII (1933), 93-113. "Unlike the irresponsible demoniac, who is kept outside the pale because his ecstasies are shallow, unreliable, and not under his own control, the poet-philosopher will draw his inspiration from the vision of the ideal world, which will enthrall him with an enduring passion" (p. 102).

[26] On Plato's theory of imitation, see W. J. Verdenius, *Mimesis: Plato's Doctrine of Artistic Imitation and Its Meaning to Us* (Leiden, 1949); Yvonne Grand, *Recherche des principes d'une philosophie des arts dits d'imitation chez Platon, Aristote et Plotin* (Dissertation, Université de Fribourg, Switzerland, 1952); A. Diès, *Autour de Platon*, 2 vols. (Paris, 1927), pp. 594ff.

[27] Cf. Croissant, *Aristote et les mystères*, pp. 18-19; *Phaedrus* 244a ff.; *Apology* 21b ff.; *Meno* 99; *Laws* 791b, 790e.

[28] Cf. Aristotle, *Eudemian Ethics* 1225a27 ff. Also, Croissant, *op. cit.*, p. 29.

is the result of his melancholic temperament; it is not unusual, and it is an outward manifestation of an inward condition which can be explained in accordance with principles of medicine. Thus Aristotle too denies any supernatural influence in bringing about this condition.

But it is still possible that the enthusiast does have real knowledge, even if he acquires it in dubious ways. The point is that the man who is "inspired," such as the poet, must have a guide for his creative work if he is to produce anything other than superficial, misleading, and emotionally cheap stories. The poet can possess skill and knowledge; the *Poetics,* seen from this point of view, lays down the conditions for the knowing poet to meet in constructing his work of art, as opposed to the ignorant and merely enthusiastic poet.[29] The poet who composes a tragic drama in accordance with the proper principles first must be possessed of knowledge himself and, second, must produce a sequence of emotional states in his audience which is a condition for the transmission of knowledge.

In what sense can it be said that the experience of witnessing a tragic drama is one in which knowledge is gained? We have seen that one interpretation of catharsis is a quasi-cognitive one, claiming that catharsis refers to a process in which some intellectual apprehension is achieved: the beholder sees into, as it were, the nature of fear and pity, or human destiny, or the like. This view maintains that when the tragedy is a good one the audience comes to "see" or "know" something that it did not see or know before. We have also pointed out that the *Oresteia* is a drama in which positions are stated and argued for. Presumably, the audience witnessing this drama would come away with knowledge that it did not possess before.

There is evidence in writing other than the *Poetics* that Aristotle could quite properly regard the dramatic experience as one

[29] That the poet is apt to be melancholic is asserted in the *Problems* (the authenticity of which is questioned): "Why is it that all men who are outstanding in philosophy, poetry, or the arts are melancholic, and some to such an extent that they are infected by the diseases arising from black bile, as the story of Heracles among the heroes tells? . . . All melancholic persons are abnormal, not by disease but by nature" (953a; 955a [tr. W. S. Hett], Loeb Library).

in which knowing occurred. This is implied in the *De Anima* where the difference between sensation and knowledge is claimed to be that the former apprehends only individuals, while the latter apprehends universals, and that these can be said to reside in the soul.[30] But in order that the soul may know, it must be free of all impurities:

> The thinking part of a soul must therefore be, while impassible, capable of receiving the form of an object; that is, must be potentially identical in character with its object without being the object. Mind must be related to what is thinkable, as sense is to what is sensible. Therefore, since everything is a possible object of thought, mind . . . must be pure from all admixture; for the co-presence of what is alien to its nature is a hindrance and a block. . . .[31]

The impediment to the knowing part of the soul (the mind) would include emotions such as those which are aroused by the tragic drama. The "catharsis of such emotions" could then refer to the fact that the soul, in order to know, has to be freed from the inhibiting power of such emotions.

Aristotle accepted the common belief of his time that the soul could be freed from emotions.[32] In the general case, this was thought of as a freeing from a certain kind of madness, ecstasy (ἔκστασις). And this condition, as we have already noted, is the consequence of a melancholy temperament.[33] A common, and

[30] *De Anima* II, 5. 417b 20-24.

[31] *De Anima* III, 4. 429a 14-21 (tr. J. A. Smith).

[32] Both Pythagorean and Hippocratic writings affirm this belief, as do the dialogues of Plato.

[33] Cf. Croissant, "Aristote et les mystères," pp. 34-47, especially p. 44: "L'extatique est l'esclave de son tempérament physiologique et cela l'explique tout entier. C'est dans la même esprit qu'Aristote définit l'enthousiasme, dans la *Politique,* comme un πάθος τοῦ περὶ τὴν ψυχὴν ἤθους (1340a 11-12). A ce titre, l'enthousiasme dépend de la partie inférieure de l'âme, l'ὀρεκτικόν. Il y voisine avec les autres passions, comme la pitié et la crainte, et des dispositions moins transitoires qui sont les 'manières d'être' (ἕξεις). La *Politique* met en effet l'enthousiasme sur le même pied que la pitié et la crainte et ceux qui y sont sujets rentrent avec les individus prédisposés à la pitié (ἐλεήμονες) ou à la crainte (φοβητικοί), dans la catégoire des passionnés (παθητικοί)" (1342a 5-7; 12).*

＊ "The ecstatic man is the slave of his physiological temperament and that explains him entirely. In that spirit Aristotle defines enthusiasm in the *Politics* as a πάθος τοῦ περὶ τὴν ψυχὴν ἤθους [a certain emotion concerning the character of

seemingly efficacious treatment for melancholia, as Aristotle noted, was music. He accepts it as a powerful means of restoring the soul to its proper harmony, in which the mind dominates, and in which emotions that obstruct moral vision are removed. Does not music have some influence over a man's character?

> It must have such an influence if characters are affected by it. And that they are so affected is proved in many ways, and not the least by the power which the songs of Olympus exercise; for beyond question they inspire enthusiasm, and enthusiasm is an emotion of the ethical part of the soul. . . . Rhythm and melody supply imitations of anger and gentleness, and also of courage and temperance, and of all the qualities contrary to these, and of the other qualities of character, which hardly fall short of the actual affections, as we know from our own experience, for in listening to such strains our souls undergo a change. The habit of feeling pleasure or pain at mere representation is not far removed from the same feeling about realities. . . .[34]

That it does have such an influence is supported by the observation of the change it in fact effects in people; and by the general principle that an imitation produces consequences very like the effect of the original. Music is a mode of imitation of temperamental states. Its efficacy as a restorative to the proper functioning of the soul is finally affirmed in this way:

> For feelings such as pity and fear, or, again, enthusiasm, exist very strongly in some souls, and have more or less influence over all. Some persons fall into a religious frenzy, whom we see as a result of the sacred melodies—when they have used the melodies that excite the soul to mystic frenzy—restored as though they had found healing and purgation. Those who are influenced by pity or fear, and every emotional nature, must have a like experience, and others in so far as each is susceptible to such emotions, and all are in a manner purged and their souls lightened and delighted.[35]

---

the soul (1304a 11-12)]. Accordingly, enthusiasm belongs to the lower part of the soul, the ὀρεκτικόν [appetites]. It is close to the other passions such as pity and fear, and the less transient dispositions which are the 'characteristics of being' (ἕξεις). The *Politics* puts enthusiasm on the same footing as pity and fear, and those who are subject to it are to be classified with those predisposed to pity (ἐλεήμονες) or fear (φοβητικοί) in the general class of those who suffer strong emotion (παθητικοί)" (1342a 5-7; 12).

[34] *Politics* VIII, 5. 1340a 9-12 (tr. Jowett).
[35] *Politics* VIII, 7. 1342a 6-16 (tr. Jowett).

This last remark suggests that the imitative arts produce a great variety of conditions in the soul: music can produce frenzy as well as restore the enthusiast to a state of tranquility. The difference in the effect of the music depends on the kind of melody it is, i.e., what temperamental state it is imitative of. The same undoubtedly applies to the other modes of imitation mentioned in the opening of the *Poetics*. But while music is imitative of emotional states, the drama is imitative of human actions. This means one ought to expect a more complicated and morally more profound effect from the drama than from music.

In the case of the religious enthusiasts mentioned in the *Politics*, music has the effect of tranquilizing them; it induces calm where before there was agitation. Yet the religious enthusiast claims to have had a specific kind of noetic experience: he has been inspired by the god, has been vouchsafed knowledge of ultimate things, and has finally been delivered from his fear of suffering and annihilation. Now Aristotle wishes to point out that although there are similarities between this kind of process and that which we observe and experience in the theater, they are fundamentally different. For in the latter case it is correct to say that there has been a knowing activity, while in the former it is not. In other words, he is countering the claims of the religious enthusiast with the claims of a confirmed lover of the theater. But why does he do this? Because he wishes to show, on moral and political grounds, that the tragic drama is beneficial to the *polis*, while the excesses of the religious enthusiast are not. In this contention he is, indeed, countering Plato who maintained that all forms of enthusiasm are suspect and to be discouraged. In sum then, Aristotle wishes to maintain that (1) the condition of enthusiasm is general and widespread, especially among men of unusual gifts (poets, philosophers, artists); (2) this condition is frequently dealt with by means of the excesses which follow upon the exercises of the religious enthusiast; (3) there is, finally, a better and politically justifiable, and indeed intellectually sound, way of dealing with enthusiasm by means of the tragic drama.

Since this is his contention, we must discover what it is that the tragic drama effects which allows us to say that it is morally and politically enlightening and useful.

When we think of the variety that exists among the Greek dramas that have come down to us, and the still greater variety that would have been known by Aristotle, it is difficult to believe that he, any more than a present day critic, would have intended to assume that the object of representation would be alike in all tragedies. Rather, many kinds of imitations, many dissimilar dramatic situations with their corresponding responses in the audience would be encountered by the observer. Yet Aristotle, with his passion for classification, was able to discern something in the tragic drama which was akin to that which he observed in the mystery religions, as well as a set of distinctive characteristics which only tragedy possessed.

Aristotle's point in *Poetics,* Chapters Three and Four, is that tragedy is the culmination of an organic-like development from primitive bucolic religious celebrations. Tragedy comes later, hence is more developed, more fully realizes its form, than the earlier stages do. Consequently it is better in the same sense that an adult is better than a child. There is a developmental principle in the evolving forms of drama, for the later grow out of the earlier; but there is also a functional principle, for every stage aims at an end which will be more fully realized by tragedy proper than by the earlier dithyrambic satyr dance. It is a revolutionary insight to regard an art form as having an etiology. In saying this it is evident that Aristotle was aware of something that recent anthropologists and cultural historians have overlooked when they claim that Greek religious ritual and tragedy are similar. They are similar, not simply because of a generic principle, as these interpreters have sometimes claimed, but because of a functional principle: they are alike because they perform a similar function, and this Aristotle saw. Catharsis is his term to describe this function which is essential to both the imitative arts and the religious celebrations of the enthusiasts.

But there is obviously a profound difference between celebrating the life and death of a god and going to see a tragic drama in the theater. An awareness of what the difference is is essential to understanding why Aristotle thought the tragic drama was morally justifiable while the orgiastic mystery celebrations were not. In the tragic drama there is a real object that the emotions are attached to: there is a plot and a hero. The tragic drama makes available to the beholder an imitation constructed in accordance with a set of principles, namely those elaborated in the *Poetics;* and this object is then apprehended by a combination of activities which Aristotle called perceiving (αἴσθησις), imagining (φαντασία), and thinking (διάνοια).

The imitation is an object of perception insofar as it consists of individual objects and events apprehended by means of the particular senses. In addition, the drama is apprehended as the product of the poet's capacity to imagine, to entertain images not necessarily related to reality.[36] And yet the poet's created images are taken as something more than mere phantasy, for they arouse affective states and are considered to be true or false, i.e., dramatically plausible or implausible, and therefore believable or unbelievable. Now in the *De Anima* Aristotle maintains that the work of the imagination as such is without affect unless there is belief attached to it:

> For imagination is different from either perceiving or discursive thinking, though it is not found without sensation, or judgment without it. That this activity is not the same kind of thinking judgment is obvious. For imagining lies within our own power whenever we wish (e.g., we can call up a picture, as in the practice of mnemonics by the use of mental images), but in forming opinions we are not free: we cannot escape the alternative of falsehood or truth. Further, when we think something to be fearful or threatening, emotion is immediately produced, and so too with what is encouraging; but when we merely imagine we remain unaffected as persons who are looking at a painting of some dreadful or encouraging scene.[37]

If the tragic events were taken as merely the work of imagination they would not necessarily arouse emotions. But they do arouse emotions, and they are accepted as exhibits of conditions that are of vital concern to the audience. Therefore the faculty of rational belief is brought into play. Mind, the thinking and judging aspect

[36] It must be remembered that Aristotle uses imagination (φαντασία) in two senses: (1) as that faculty of the soul which organizes and interprets the perceived objects; (2) as that faculty which can function without the stimulus of a sensible object, hence can create images.

[37] *De Anima* III, 3. 427b 15-25 (tr. J. A. Smith).

of the soul, is operative in the experience of watching a tragic drama.[38]

The drama is an object of knowledge as well as an imaginative construction because the audience is led to make a judgment about the truth or falsity of what is depicted. Now the drama can be said to be "true" insofar as it is a good imitation; and insofar as it is a set of events plausible in itself. As a more or less adequate imitation of the human situation it can state or fail to state what is true about human action; truth and falsity are properly predicated of it, if it is based on some kind of "objective" occurrence.[39] But the poet is not the historian; he aims at something philosophical, not simply factual. Yet he has a source of what might be called "philosophical history," namely the myths and legends of the past. Aristotle asserts that the poet ought to work with these, although he is free to alter them in certain ways:

> That is the reason why the subjects of tragedy are, as we said some time ago, provided by a few families. By chance rather than intent, poets found the way to provide these situations in their plots, and this forces them to go to those families which were thus afflicted.[40]

Secondly, the drama can be "true" insofar as it is fully realized as a plausible set of events in its presentation. As Else points out, it is not the case that the poet ought to take the impossible as against the possible. The necessary condition to be met is plausibility, and if the impossible, i.e., what would not happen according to the natural order of events, is more plausible in a specific instance, then its use is justified. If the poet can combine the plausible and the possible he has the best situation for tragic drama.[41] Such drama provides a plot through which the hero

[38] Cf. *De Anima* III, 4.

[39] Cf. *Metaphysics* V, 29. 1024b 26-27. "A false account, in so far as it is false, is the account of things that are not. Hence, every account is false which is an account of something other than that of which it is true; for example, an account of a circle is false of a triangle" (tr. Richard Hope).

[40] *Poetics* 14. 1454a 9-10 (tr. Grube). Cf. 9. 1451b 15-26.

[41] The passage in the *Poetics* is: "What is impossible but can be believed should be preferred to what is possible but unconvincing. The plot should not consist of inexplicable incidents; as far as possible it should contain nothing inexplicable" (1460a 27-30, tr. Grube).

comes to see certain fundamental truths about himself and by extension about mankind in general. The truths which the drama makes available can be grasped only if the soul is free to know, that is, if *nous* can function. And it can if the emotions of pity and fear are controlled. But what the beholder comes to know in this way is psychologically very difficult to accept. That is, the deliverances of the drama are not easily assimilated and carried away. They can be accepted by the man of unusual strength of character (the philosopher). But they can hardly be accepted by the average person, for they are terrifying and disconcerting. Further, as Aristotle emphasizes over and over again, man is not simply a knower: he is a social being. Now, the outcome of the apprehension of dramatic truths is to know something of great importance and generality, but by this knowledge to be injured socially, or at least made less accepting of the political and moral demands placed upon one as a social being. The knowledge of what one is and what the human condition is (assuming this is of the order of truths revealed by tragic drama) is something the average man cannot cope with, for that knowledge is disturbing, as we have said, to all but the true philosopher. Thus the effect of tragic drama must be something more than the revelation of a truth, no matter how profound that truth may be. It must prepare the spectator to know that truth and to deal with the effect such knowledge will have. The process which is referred to as catharsis is an indispensable means to the acceptance of this truth, for it embraces a sequence of emotional states which conduct the beholder through a concern for self to an acceptance of the guilty hero. It places him in a position to understand the role of the *polis* in the reconciliation which must be accorded such men.[42]

In its pedagogical function the drama coerces the audience into recognizing the nature of cosmic events and purposes: to witness

[42] Aristotle suggests that the city can properly sponsor the dramatic festivals, because in so doing it solidifies and, as it were, explains its own function. It can use the drama not simply as a means of pacification, but also as a means of teaching its citizens that those, such as Orestes and Oedipus, and by extension the beholder, are received into the city. This is accomplished either by direct presentation of the fact, as in the *Oresteia*, or by inductive analogy, as in the *Oedipus Rex*, where the audience accords this to the hero.

the *Oresteia,* for example, is to be brought face to face with a story of the past which makes statements about one's innermost concerns and provides answers to one's most intimate questions. But to make the statements and answer the questions something more than mere exhibition is needed: the pertinence and the power of the vision must be recognized. The dramatic "argument" is not one that convinces through its deductive rigor; rather, it persuades through its emotional effect. And that effect is what is summed up under the concept of catharsis.

The process by means of which the audience comes to share the poet's knowledge depends, then, first upon the quality of imitation which the drama presents, and secondly upon the catharsis which it effects.

I have said that the audience comes to know what the poet knows, for the tragedy he writes makes known to the beholder a paradigmatic situation in which the anxieties and fears of men, the nature of fate and suffering, are given specific content. The mere story of Orestes becomes "real" at the hands of Aeschylus in the same way that the mere story of Christ (paradigmatic for Western civilization at another time) becomes "real" when embodied in a passion play. Let us call this the "analogical function" of drama, because it can be considered, from this point of view, as mediating between the individual beholder and a paradigmatic situation.

Now Aristotle is, among other things, inquiring into the analogical function of the tragic drama. And he maintains that there is a fundamental difference between the effectiveness of tragedy in this capacity, and the enthusiastic states of the religious ecstatics. The tragic drama effects a knowing, while the daimonomania of the celebrants does not. In both cases certain strong emotions are induced; but in the tragic drama these emotions are related to specific acts performed before the audience. The means here is not identification with the hero, in the same sense that there is identification with the god in the ceremony of initiation, although there is at first identification with the hero. But this is followed by a different attitude, namely a distancing, a feeling *about* the entire situation, no longer a feeling along with the hero in his tribulation. The difference could be stated by reference to the culmination of the religious celebration and the culmination of the dramatic experience. In the first the initiate takes the god into himself (incorporation) and thereby shares the powers and properties of the god, most important of which is immortality. In the second the participant comes to accept the hero as he really is, namely as a man with a particular character and logic of action, and by extension comes to accept himself *as he is,* not as he would wish to be. The former then culminates in a wish fulfillment; the latter in a recognition of the nature of reality.[43] The former cannot be said, for this reason, to give knowledge, while the latter can be said to give knowledge. But the knowledge is something the audience can accept only because of the sequence of emotional states it has been led through.

This sequence involves first the experiencing of pity and fear and then the "purification" or allaying of these emotions. What this means can only be understood in the light of the conditions which arouse pity and fear in the dramatic situation.

The way in which Aristotle conceived of pity and fear is made clear in the *Rhetoric:*

> fear is caused by whatever we feel has great power of destroying us, or of harming us in ways that tend to cause us great pain. Hence the very indications of such things are terrible, making us feel that the terrible thing itself is close at hand; the approach of what is terrible is just what we mean by 'danger.' Such indications are the enmity and anger of people who have power to do something to us; for it is plain that they have the will to do it, and so they are on the point of doing it. Also injustice in possession of power; for it is the unjust man's will to do evil that makes him unjust.[44]

---

[43] This contrast is made with psychoanalytic theory specifically in mind. Freud saw both religious celebrations and tragedy as wish-fulfilling experiences. It is difficult to square Freud's aesthetic theory with the kinds of dramas we are discussing here. Wish-fulfilling phantasies are entertained when the secondary processes are submerged, as it were, by the primary. But tragedy insists, as Aristotle saw, that the secondary processes be allowed to function. Certainly the tragic poet has a much stronger "sense of reality," in Freud's meaning of the phrase, than does the religious enthusiast.

[44] *Rhetoric* II, 5. 1382a 28-1382b (tr. W. Rhys Roberts).

There follows a list of situations that arouse fear, and then this conclusion:

> All terrible things are more terrible if they give us no chance of retrieving a blunder—either no chance at all, or only one that depends on our enemies and not ourselves. Those things are also worse which we cannot, or cannot easily, help. Speaking generally, anything causes us to feel fear that when it happens to, or threatens, others causes us to feel pity.[45]

The tragic hero is one who cannot retrieve a blunder, and who cannot easily help the kind of thing that he performs. He is the person who, pre-eminently, would feel fear, and this is communicated to the audience by his words, his bearing, the music and the spectacle of the tragedy. Empathetically one would feel fear also. Yet it is someone else who is suffering; consequently one feels pity for him, especially with the realization that it is a "story" about a man, not oneself that suffers in just that way.

"Pity," Aristotle remarks, "may be defined as a feeling of pain caused by the sight of some evil, destructive or painful, which befalls one who does not deserve it, and which we might expect to befall ourselves or some friend of ours, and moreover to befall us soon." [46] However, in order to feel pity, "we must also believe in the goodness of at least some people; if you think nobody good, you will believe that everybody deserves evil fortune." [47] The situation most likely to arouse pity exists when those afflicted with evil "heighten the effect of their words with suitable gestures, tones, dress, and dramatic action generally . . . they thus put the disasters before our eyes and make them seem close to us, just coming or just past." [48]

From this it follows that the kind of knowledge gained through witnessing a well-composed drama is directly about human affairs and our attitudes toward one another as human beings living in a political organization. It is not knowledge about immortality or

[45] *Ibid.* 1382b 23-27.
[46] *Ibid.* II, 8. 1385b 12-16.
[47] *Ibid.* 1385b 35-1386a 2.
[48] *Ibid.* 1386a 31-1386b.

salvation or some divine "other" in the universe. Further, the knowledge is crucial to us as men: since we assume that there are good people in the world and wish them well, we must come to understand why the goodness is not self-sufficient, not dependable as a guarantee for human happiness. The tragic drama asserts that conditions over which we have little or no control often bring about harsh sufferings to those upon whom the guilt of violence and unreason falls; and that a view of such catastrophes which enables men to achieve self-control and mastery over their fears is essential to the attainment of a noble character. In short, the philosophic life, the best possible for man, is only possible if the emotions aroused by human suffering (our own included) are brought under the control of reason. In making this possible, the tragic drama repairs defects in uncultivated human nature.

Tragedy, like all other forms of human making, exists as a means of repairing the shortcomings of nature. It seems to be the case that Aeschylus agrees with Plato and Aristotle in maintaining that tragic drama can be instrumental in repairing the deficiencies of the *polis* which arise from the primitive demands of man's irrational self. The organization of society under rulers, the moral commandments of the state and the religion, the development of the law court, are all means of repairing the great ravages of human irrationality. We must add to those another means, the tragic drama. Clearly the *Oresteia* serves this function, for it not only exhibits the achievements of one moral and political organization over another, as well as one set of religious beliefs over another, but it is itself the means of impressing the audience with the success and the goodness of that achievement. The drama then is one manifestation of human *techné* which must be seriously considered in terms of the function it performs, and when it is so considered it is judged to be superior to the previous and competing means to arrive at the same ends.

As a species of art, the drama partly completes and partly imitates nature:

> Now intelligent action is for the sake of an end; therefore the nature of things also is so. Thus if a house, e.g., had been a thing made by nature, it would have been made in the same way as it is now by

art; and if things made by nature were made also by art, they would come to be in the same way as by nature. Each step then in the series is for the sake of the next; and generally art partly completes what nature cannot bring to a finish, and partly imitates her.[49]

This completion and imitation is the result of thinking which gives rise to making:

> it is by art that those products come whose form dwells in the mind, where by "form" I mean what it is to be that product, its first or primary being. . . . One phase of the productive process, therefore, is called "thinking," and another, "making": that which proceeds from the starting point and from the form is "thinking"; that which proceeds from the end point of the thinking is "making." [50]

Man, because he has a mind, because he can think, can guide his making activity to the reparation of the deficiencies in nature. This in turn requires some sense of how things ought to be, and this is possible because a "form dwells in the mind."

What then must the artist have in his mind to be a good "technician"? What must he know in order to assure competence to his making? The technical competence that the poet must possess is made clear from the discussion in the *Poetics*, especially the much neglected Chapter Twenty-five in which mistakes of criticism are briefly set down. But more important than that is the knowledge he must command. This is only alluded to in the *Poetics*, but is supplied in fact in the moral and metaphysical treatises. Thus the poet must understand the limits of possibility and probability, what is to be sought morally, and what constitutes consistency in action.[51]

He must understand what a good man is, and he must present a hero who is a morally good man, not one who is depraved or simply ignorant of what he is doing. If the poet does not understand this and presents a man who is not virtuous in some degree, the resulting drama is hateful. The emotions of pity and fear will not be produced and dealt with properly. From an examination of the

---

[49] *Physics* II, 8. 199a 12-17 (tr. R. P. Hardie and R. K. Gaye).
[50] *Metaphysics* VII, 7. 1032a 30-1032b 3; 1032b 15-18 (tr. Richard Hope).
[51] Cf. *Poetics* 25, esp. 1461b 9-25.

words Aristotle uses to characterize the good man who is the tragic hero [52] it is evident that by a good man he means one who is *morally good,* i.e., equitable, honest, and capable of making moral decisions in pursuit of a moral purpose.[53] And further, it is essential that the poet present the hero as not responsible in the usual sense for what he has done.

Aristotle argues that it is better to present an action in which the hero is ignorant of the true nature of the act, than one in which he acts knowingly. The latter kind of deed was preferred by the older poets.[54] The difficulty with their presentations was that they could in no way condone or excuse what the hero had done.[55]

In the case of Orestes, the mitigating circumstance is not ignorance, but the fact that he is directed by the will of another, i.e., Apollo. Yet Orestes, like the tragic hero, is one who is responsible for his action. And one of the purposes of the tragic resolution is to present the ways in which blameworthy action done out of ignorance or through coercion can be dealt with.

There is no doubt but that these are difficult, almost impossible problems; yet the tragic poet must know about and have adequate solutions for them if his work is to be more than mere entertainment or at worst a danger to the audience.

The playwrights and philosophers who concern us believed the dramatic experience is one in which the insight and intellectual power of the craftsman is somehow conveyed to the beholder by the created product of his skill. Thus the ability the poet has to repair the deficiencies in nature makes nature more complete and

[52] Cf. *Poetics* 13 and 15.

[53] For a discussion of these passages and a determination of what Aristotle means by the "good man," see Charles H. Reeves, "The Aristotelian Concept of the Tragic Hero," *Amer. Journ. Philol.,* LXXIII (1952), 172-88.

[54] *Poetics* 14. 1453b 24-29.

[55] I. M. Glanville comments: "Aristotle's reasons for disapproving the second type of tragic act, preferred by the ancients, have now become explicit. Since the condition of pity is that the hero shall be ἀνάξιος [undeserving of evil] and not come to misery διὰ μοχθηρίαν [through depravity] the poet must, like the advocate, suggest some way of condoning his behavior, by presenting him as not in the ordinary sense responsible for his action" ("Tragic Error," *Class. Quart.,* XLIII [1949], 50).

more understandable for those who lack his gifts; just as the ability of the good shoemaker or shipbuilder makes nature more complete for the user of these items, and the product of the good statesman makes the life of the citizen a better one. Without these human contributions, nature would indeed offer only a partial resolution of our practical and theoretical concerns.

The technical competence of the poet is tested by his ability to present a plot which has a specific emotional and noetic effect upon the audience. These are consequences of the drama as imitation. For both Plato and Aristotle art is to be considered an "imitation." It is obvious from the way they use the term that it had a variety of meanings for them; but two fundamental meanings may be distinguished in the writings of each. Plato took great care to assert that imitation could be of two kinds: 1) εἰκαστική, an art which produces something that may at first seem to be different from its original, but is really like or similar to it in essential form, 2) φανταστική, art which produces mere fantasies, that appear to be like the original but are not. The first is produced by the man who has knowledge in the Platonic sense of knowing the essential form of reality; the second is produced by the ignorant or deceiving man who either cannot get beyond the realm of appearances, or uses his art to mislead the unknowing. This distinction is clearly drawn in the *Sophist*.[56]

Obviously, the good dramatist is one who imitates by means of his knowledge of reality and therefore produces εἰκαστική. We might refer to Plato's theory of imitation as idealistic, in the sense that the good imitation is one which follows the realm of ideal forms. But we will see that Aristotle's theory of imitation, then, is idealistic too because for him art can be said to be an imitation of the way things ought to be. The difference between the two interpretations of mimesis concerns where the norm is to be found. For Aristotle it is found in closely observing the order of nature. Art is an imitation necessarily, and a transformation in

[56] 236ff. See Cornford's discussion of this passage in *Plato's Theory of Knowledge*, pp. 195ff. Also the following excellent discussions of J. Tate: "Imitation in Plato's Republic," *Class. Quart.*, XXII (1928), 16-23; "Plato and 'Imitation,'" *ibid.*, XXVI (1932), 161-69; "On Plato: *Laws* X 889cd," *ibid.*, XXX (1936), 48-54.

that it repairs deficiencies, for as a species of *techné* it tries to follow and improve upon nature. Like nature it gives birth to beings.

In the first sense in which Aristotle uses the term "imitation," art is imitative in that it is productive, as is nature.[57] All things that come into being are produced by nature, art, or accident. However, in the case of art, the maker is free to choose the matter to be worked on, while nature is not.[58] Furthermore, each natural being has a principle of movement within itself, while artificial beings find their principle of movement, their form, in the mind of the artist.[59] There is a difference, also, in the final cause, for nature is itself its own final cause, while the product of art finds its final cause in something external to itself.

In the second sense in which art is an "imitation" for Aristotle he refers to the fact that we find events in art of the sort we find in everyday experience. Here Plato and Aristotle differ in their evaluation of imitation, for the fact that art imitates "appearances" is used in a derogatory way by Plato, while it is used in a commendatory way by Aristotle, as long as the events depicted are carefully selected and properly organized.

But it may be legitimate to suggest a third meaning of imitation in which Plato and Aristotle would be in agreement. Art is imitation in the sense that it produces something akin to what is produced by the enthusiastic states of religious frenzy. That is, just as these celebrations induce and remove emotions, so art induces and removes emotions. Specifically, the tragic drama is an imitation of a good but not perfect man exhibiting his ἁμαρτία (hamartia), his ἕξις (disposition) to act in a certain way because of what he is by nature, not necessarily because of some fault which is private to him. The tragic drama is an imitation of such a man making a mistake in both knowledge and choice, yet retaining a nobility of character in the face of his adversity. And further, he finds his strength to persevere mobilizes on his side the protective forces of the city which accepts and judges him.

[57] *Metaphysics* 1032a 12-13.
[58] *Physics* 194b 8.
[59] *Physics* 192b 23-32; *Metaphysics* 1032b.

In this sense we can say that the tragic drama is imitative of the best, for it exhibits what ought to obtain politically, morally, and psychologically. But it is also true that the action of the tragic drama is not itself, nor can it ever be, of that which is morally perfect. For what is perfect in this sense cannot arouse emotion. In the tragedy, should only perfection of form and right reason for all action be exhibited, no pity and fear would be aroused. Only some disparity, injustice, disproportion in human behavior and its rewards arouses pity and fear.

It is on this ground that the difference in Plato's and Aristotle's theory of imitation can be clearly seen. For Plato the fact that tragedy can exist only if it represents what is unjust in some sense makes it superfluous to the good community. Drama can only be justified on therapeutic grounds or in terms of the expediency of political control. It may be practically useful; it can never be philosophically beneficial. For Aristotle it is useful, but beyond that it is philosophically justified, for what to Plato is its imperfection is indeed a proper imitation of what is. For Plato no imperfection ought to be imitated; for Aristotle imperfection must be imitated because it is a way to knowledge, and through the imitation we can refashion the reality.

The fundamental difference between Plato and Aristotle in their analysis rests not so much on theoretical grounds as on pedagogical grounds. They agree that the drama is a means by which the poet can transmit knowledge to his audience. Plato doubts that the poet can know, since he is usually a mere mouthpiece of his muse. But assuming he can know, and Plato admits there are good poets, then Plato still finds it difficult to accept the poet as an adequate teacher. For him, it is a matter of the poet *or* the philosopher, and he believes the philosopher better equipped to instruct the citizen, for the philosopher is versed in matters of statecraft and virtue. For Aristotle, on the other hand, the poet is well equipped to perform a pedagogical function provided he has knowledge, something Aristotle believes he can have, and knows how to put a play together, something he can learn. Here it is a choice of the poet or the historian; and there is no doubt but that the poet says things in a way calculated to instill truths about men and the city, while the historian is limited to immediate actions with reference to specific events.[60]

The two philosophers agree, however, that the tragic drama is a possible means to moral and political well-being. Art is an activity which exists for something beyond the mere appearance it provides. To the audience this may be pleasure, but when Aristotle speaks of the "pleasure peculiar to tragedy" he means the pleasure which accompanies the insight into the general human situation. Both he and Plato would have the drama express universals of this kind; but they have different views of the kind of person the good poet is, and the image each unconsciously conveys is, to be sure, an image of himself. To Plato the trustworthy poet is a philosopher with a daimon who allows him to speak the truth. Socrates would be a tragic poet for he has the gift of the genius. Indeed, for Plato the poet should be "a man of genius—a philosopher and an enthusiast whose influence would be good for the old as well as the young." [61] For Aristotle the poet should be a man sober and untouched by the wild visions of ecstatic states. Indeed, he will most likely be a melancholic type but he must control his tendency to enthusiasm in order to speak the truth.[62]

---

[60] "A poet differs from a historian . . . because the historian relates what happened, the poet what might happen. That is why poetry is more akin to philosophy and is a better thing than history; poetry deals with general truths, history with specific events" (*Poetics* 9. 1451b 1-7, tr. Grube).

[61] J. Tate, "Plato and 'Imitation,'" p. 167.

[62] See Aristotle *Problems* XXX, 1. 954b 20. Also Croissant, "Aristote et les mystères," pp. 110-11. "Dans la théorie de la catharsis, l'observation psychologique, menée en toute liberté, s'est ainsi trouvée en accord, dans ses conclusions, avec les désirs du philosophe soucieux des fins dernières. Aristote le dit lui-même dans la *Politique:* quand ils ne nuisent pas, les plaisirs, servent la fin dernière autant que le délassement. Le plaisir que donne le théâtre est de ceux-là: Aristote y insiste quelques pages plus loin, dans le passage relatif à la théorie de la catharsis. C'etait aussi le cas pour les mystères. Ils n'avaient aucune influence proprement moralisatrice, mais leur utilité n'était pas seulement d'ordre psychologique et physiologique. Pour mieux dire, par leur seul rôle psychologique, ils servaient l'idéal moral du philosophe. Ils travaillaient à assurer chez l'homme l'équilibre de la matière psychique, sans lequel tout équilibre moral est impossible." ("In the theory of catharsis, an unbiased psychological inquiry is in agreement in its conclusions with the wishes of the thoughtful philosopher as he considers ultimate human purposes. Aris-

The philosophers agree, however, that the tragic drama is a kind of imitation with serious moral and political consequences. The audience is witness to an action in which the community is forced to make a judgment, for the hero is one who has committed an offense against the citizens and the *polis*. A way is found to deal with a man like Orestes or Oedipus. The fear that results from man's natural anxiety about his destiny is perhaps allayed, but it is not permanently stilled. Only for an Orestes or an Oedipus, those who become heroes in the supernatural sense, can it be removed. For a release from this anxiety the mortal must find another way.

One is to live the life of the wise man, to achieve the harmony of soul of which Plato speaks in the *Republic;* to become the man who is "great-souled" as Aristotle says in the *Nicomachean Ethics.* But this is not a condition easily gained; most men lack the stamina and the intelligence to achieve it.

The second way is by means of an external, imposed discipline rather than an internal discipline. This is what the audiences at the dramatic festivals were offered. The dramatic festival was a group experience; the audience was the citizenry of the *polis* administered to by the spectacle which controlled this momentary organization. The little world of spectacle effected a knowledge and a harmony in the citizens which would have its permanent consequences, if properly utilized.

Tragedy could only succeed if it enforced the belief one would naturally hold about the goodness of men; if it demonstrated that one's natural feelings of pity were justified, and that one's feelings of fear need not follow upon pity. Fear need not follow pity because through the drama one could come to understand the in-

---

totle says it himself in the *Politics:* where pleasures are not harmful, they realize ultimate ends as much as recreation. The pleasure which the theater provides is of that kind: Aristotle insists upon it several pages further on, in the passage bearing on the theory of catharsis. That was also so in regard to the mysteries. They have no moralizing influence properly speaking, but their usefulness was not only of a psychological and physiological kind. It is more correct to say that in their psychological function they served the moral ideal of the philosopher. In man they worked to effect the psychological equilibrium without which all moral balance is impossible.")

evitability of fate, and to realize that those who have been caught in its net can find, if not expiation, at least a reconciliation with the community of men.

Now if we return to a consideration of the *Oresteia* in the light of this discussion, we will see that this drama deals with the problem of reconciliation and of catharsis differently from most other dramas of the Athenian playwrights. In the *Oresteia,* considered as the story of Orestes, the committing of a wrong and reconciliation are a part of the plot itself. Orestes has taken the life of his mother and has suffered for it; but at the end he is pardoned. It might be said that in the *Oresteia* reconciliation is realized within the drama itself. The audience is led to behold the action of a man who feels that he bears the guilt for his own and his family's wrongdoings; it sees him succeed with divine help in becoming free of his guilt, for he is able to return to the city (specifically, his city of Argos) and assume the place of leadership rightfully his.

This kind of action is unusual if compared with the tragic pattern enunciated by Aristotle as the best. In the *Oresteia* the pity and fear aroused in the audience are dissipated by the ending. The hero has not suffered a reversal from good to bad fortune, but rather from guilt and madness to atonement, and reconciliation; the catharsis is part of the plot itself.

In contrast to the *Oresteia* stands the plot of the drama most admired by Aristotle, Sophocles' *Oedipus Rex*. Aristotle could select the latter as his prime example of tragedy precisely because catharsis does not take place objectively as a part of the action. The only sense in which catharsis can occur is as a part of the audience's response to the action. At the conclusion of the drama there is no god, no Areopagus, no city that forgives and accepts the hero. He stands before the audience as a man whose offense is the most horrible, and yet he is a man who is neither scorned nor reviled. Clearly there is a fundamental difference between the *Oresteia* and the *Oedipus Rex*. According to Aristotle's definition of tragedy only the latter could properly be called a tragedy while the former, though serious drama, is a species that I would call the "polity play" to contrast it with the "morality play" of Christian tradition.

The chief difference on Aristotle's grounds is the locus of the process he terms catharsis. In the *Oresteia* the plot is so constructed that the audience sees the hero reconciled with his community, forgiven for his wrongdoing; it is a "happy ending." In the *Oedipus Rex* the hero achieves full knowledge of his guilt and in the end stands in need of reconciliation and forgiveness, if that is in any way possible. In this kind of drama Aristotle maintains that the catharsis occurs in the audience; that the effect of witnessing this kind of tragedy is the mitigation of feelings of pity and fear.

Both Orestes and Oedipus are men who suffer the pollution of wrongdoing, who sustain with complete self-knowledge the guilt of their actions. Both are guilty, not of evil acts which were the result of forethought and calculation, but of acts forced upon them by powers outside themselves that they could not control. Both stand in need of judgment and reconciliation with their communities. To Orestes this is vouchsafed; not to Oedipus.[63]

Aristotle maintains that catharsis in some sense is a part of the total dramatic situation in the *Oedipus*. The only way in which this could be plausibly maintained is that the audience neither hates nor reviles Oedipus, but comes to accept him and to confer upon him the reconciliation which in fact a hero like Orestes achieves within the drama. The audience accepts the guilty Oedipus and in doing this is freed from the powerful emotions which the drama has induced. He can be received sympathetically even with full knowledge of who he is and what he has done.

This is made possible by the fact that the audience has the proper understanding of Oedipus through an attendance on his own painful movement to self-awareness which constitutes the action. Every man can suffer as Oedipus did, and every man can

---

[63] In the *Oedipus at Colonus* the hero does achieve reconciliation. In this sense the last of Sophocles' plays is very much like the *Oresteia* and the two can be fruitfully compared. In this sense also, the *Colonus* is not a tragedy if one accepts Aristotle's narrowest definition.

draw solace from the fact that nobility is possible even in the face of such suffering. And the implication is that when nobility persists in such an extreme instance, reconciliation is accorded the sufferer, for the audience accepts the man in spite of his wrongdoing.

Thus we can conjecture that the "purification" which is part of the dramatic experience is to be found in according to Oedipus what, in fact, is accorded to Orestes in the *Oresteia* as a part of the action itself. Were the audience to sit in judgment upon Oedipus as the Areopagus sits in judgment upon Orestes, the man would be pronounced as meriting this or that punishment, deserving of this or that fate. But no such judgment is relevant or necessary. Oedipus is as far beyond such judgment as would be a god. We need say nothing because we understand all. That is the function of true tragedy. But it is not the function of serious drama of the kind which is the *Oresteia* and the *Oedipus at Colonus*. Here there is a matter of divine purpose in the founding of the *polis* which is to be revealed. That is why I would call these dramas polity plays, for the audience is instructed about the ultimate nature of the city, insofar as it can enlighten human morality.

Aristotle has selected as true tragedy those works in which the hero is not reconciled to the city as a part of the action. That choice may determine his difficult comment that "even though Euripides manages his plays badly in other respects, he obviously is the most tragic of poets." [64] Euripides, like Sophocles, wrote plays in which the audience is forced to contribute the reconciliation of which the hero stands in need. They are tragic, then, in the sense that they do effect a catharsis of the emotions they arouse. Such dramas represent the circumstance which is indeed eminently human, for men stand without the benefit of a god's pronouncement as to the right or wrong of acts committed. Men must suffer their guilt without hope of divine dispensation removing it. And it is the individual who can act nobly even in the face of overwhelming guilt who can bestow upon an audience the

---

[64] *Poetics* 13. 1453a 28-29 (tr. Grube).

"purification" of an emotional and rational equilibrium. For he asserts that one can persevere even in a universe such as this.

Oedipus is left with his guilt; yet the audience must accept him, and in so doing initiate his ultimate reconciliation. Indeed, if we can accept an Oedipus, then as members of a community we (and perhaps even the gods themselves) can accept the individual whose guilt, although oppressive, is as nothing compared to the guilt and suffering of Oedipus.

Orestes, however, appears in a very different light. He is tried and cleared of the charges brought against him by the Erinyes. Yet what he did was certainly wrong, and he bears the responsibility for the action even though directed by Apollo. One can dispute the fairness of the arguments at the trial and the final judgment; one can question whether Orestes' act was blameworthy under the circumstances; but the drama asserts the conclusion about the hero without needing the spectators' agreement or disagreement. The endeavor here, it might be said, is to institutionalize catharsis. Athena is the leader and teacher in this effort, and what she has to say to the Athenians assembled for the trial is indeed relevant to an audience attending the *Oedipus Rex*. For such an audience learns from witnessing the judgment accorded Orestes something about the judgment that ought to be accorded Oedipus. The *Oresteia* is in fact an excellent dramatic propaedeutic to all serious drama and especially to tragedy in the limited sense that Aristotle wished to establish. For the *Oresteia* is a presentation through dramatic action of the means human reason has to control the daimonic in man, and the means it has to render anxiety and guilt, an inevitable and dangerous human condition, amenable to rational control. Athena teaches that reconciliation is possible through the properly ordered *polis* in which the conscience of the individual is guided by the judgment and wisdom of the court.

Reconciliation of the guilty individual is possible not because he is deemed "innocent"—that is furthest from the decision handed down by Athena and the Areopagus—but because he is, if noble and capable of rational understanding, worthy of being accepted in the city. The *polis* which is established under the aegis of the younger gods can take all worthy men to itself, for it has learned the only way to deal with wrongdoing is to educate for nobility and teach the nature of human destiny.

Indeed, this is the great strength of civilization, and this is one of the achievements of Greek thought: the city can become the best and most just society for men. Fundamental to this is the acceptance of a man on the condition that certain moral prerequisites are met. These are met, to be sure, by the great tragic heroes, for they come to full realization of what they are as men, and the nature of what, as men, they have done. They are taken into the community because they have, despite the enormity of their wrongdoing, come to know themselves.

Perhaps it can be said that the community which accepts the great tragic heroes is all of civilized mankind, for every generation of men who live in cities justly ruled affirms its humanity in the act of accepting them. A civilized community is one that orders itself in terms of the need to understand the conditions of human beings: of fate, guilt, and the possibilities for noble action. Such a community affirms the rationality of its citizens in the face of the most violent wrongs, for men can never free themselves of the evils of unrestrained passion and the cruelties of fate.

Orestes can thus be accepted into Athens, and Athens can fulfill the promise of civilization where Troy and Argos failed. For in Athens a guilty man whose wrongs are extreme can find just judgment; and indeed both Orestes and Oedipus found an accepting community, first after their legendary homes, in Athens.

APPENDIX

APPENDIX

Comparison of Cosmic Creator, Statesman, and Artist

COSMIC CREATOR	STATESMAN	ARTIST (POET)
1. Produces an imitation of an ideal order. The paradigms are numbers and forms. When taken as a model, they provide the logical structure for a cosmos according to reason. Must cope with irrational elements.	1. Produces an imitation of what is politically best by means of law. Laws are representations of eternally just orders. If well formulated, they are the structure for a *polis* according to reason. Must cope with the irrational element of human passion; needs to control it.	1. Produces an imitation of an action of a certain kind, i.e., good and complete. The best drama is structured in accordance with a moral ideal which is the product of reason. Must cope with irrational elements in action and response of the audience.
2. The limits of possibility defined by reason. The cosmic order controlled by Justice (Dike) in impersonal sense. Necessity determines limit of all things.	2. The limits of possibility defined by the needs and goals of society, but these in turn are determined by reason. The social order controlled by justice in both cosmic and legal sense.	2. The limits of possibility defined by nature of human action, character, and thought. Seeks to establish nature of justice in human action.
3. The cosmos is well ordered when the creator uses intelligence after the model of reality.	3. The *polis* is well ordered when the statesman knows and is guided by reality.	3. The plot is well ordered (constructed) when the artist knows human nature and moral goals, as they ought to be.
	4. City is best when based on traditional laws modified to meet goals of justice as now understood.	4. Plot is best when based on traditional stories modified to meet aesthetic needs.
5. Everything irrational must be controlled.	5. Everything irrational must be controlled, excluded if possible.	5. Everything irrational must be excluded: a plausible impossibility is preferable to an implausible possibility.
6. Process of making involves a process of "separating out" (a catharsis): this necessary to isolate the best.	6. Process of making involves separating out (a catharsis). Aim is the best *polis*.	6. Process of making involves separating out, both in plot structure and in emotional response.
7. Creator's instrument is reason which effects purification.	7. Statesman's instrument is law which both embodies reason and effects purification.	7. Artist's instrument is tragic drama which has its logic, and effects purification.
Special Problems of Order and Rationality in Universe	Special Problems of Harmony and Justice in Polis	Special Problems of Art and Psychology (Melancholia)

BIBLIOGRAPHY

BIBLIOGRAPHY

A. Texts

Aeschylus. *Aeschylus,* tr. H. Weir Smyth. 2 vols. "Loeb Classical Library."

————. *Aeschylus Agamemnon,* ed. and tr. Eduard Fraenkel. 3 vols. Oxford, 1950.

————. *Aeschylus Oresteia,* tr. Richmond Lattimore. Chicago, 1953.

————. *Die Fragmente der Tragödien des Aischylos,* ed. Hans Joachim Mette. Berlin, 1959.

————. *Oresteian Trilogy,* tr. P. Vellacott. Baltimore, 1956.

————. *Tragoediae,* ed. Gilbert Murray. 2nd edition. Oxford, 1955.

Aristotle. *Aristotle on the Art of Fiction,* tr. L. J. Potts. Cambridge, 1953.

————. *Aristotle's* De Anima *in the Version of William of Moerbeke and the Commentary of St. Thomas Aquinas,* tr. Kenelm Foster and Silvester Humphries. London, 1951.

————. *Art of Rhetoric,* tr. J. H. Freese. "Loeb Classical Library."

————. *The Ethics of Aristotle,* tr. J. A. K. Thomson. Baltimore, 1953.

————. *Generation of Animals,* tr. A. L. Peck. "Loeb Classical Library."

————. *Metaphysics,* tr. H. Tredennick. "Loeb Classical Library."

————. *Natural Science, Ethics, and Nicomachean Ethics* (selections), ed. and tr. Philip Wheelwright. 2nd edition. New York, 1951.

————. *On the Soul,* tr. W. S. Hett. "Loeb Classical Library."

————. *Parts of Animals,* tr. A. L. Peck. "Loeb Classical Library."

————. *Physics,* tr. P. Wicksteed and F. M. Cornford. 2 vols. "Loeb Classical Library."

————. *Poetics,* tr. W. Hamilton Fyfe. "Loeb Classical Library."

————. *Politics,* tr. H. Rackham. "Loeb Classical Library."

————. *Problems,* tr. W. S. Hett. 2 vols. "Loeb Classical Library."

————. *Works,* ed. W. D. Ross and J. A. Smith. Oxford, 1908-1952.

Fragments. *Epigrammata Graeca,* ed. Georg Kaibel. Berlin, 1878.

————. *Die Fragmente der Vorsokratiker,* ed. Hermann Diels. Berlin, 1937.

Hesiod. *Hesiod, The Homeric Hymns and Homerica,* tr. H. G. Evelyn-White. "Loeb Classical Library."

Homer. *The Iliad,* tr. Richmond Lattimore. Chicago, 1951.

————. *The Iliad,* tr. William Morris. London, 1934.

Plato. *The Dialogues of Plato,* tr. Benjamin Jowett. 2 vols. New York, 1937.

————. *Laws,* tr. R. G. Bury. 2 vols. "Loeb Classical Library."

————. *Oeuvres complètes de Platon,* ed. and tr. Maurice Croiset. Paris, various dates.

————. *Phaedrus, Ion, Gorgias, and Symposium, with Passages from the Republic and Laws,* tr. Lane Cooper. New York, 1938.

Polybius. *The Histories,* tr. W. R. Paton. 6 vols. "Loeb Classical Library."

Sextus Empiricus. *Writings,* tr. R. G. Bury. 4 vols. "Loeb Classical Library."

B. COMMENTARY AND CRITICISM

Adkins, Arthur W. H. *Merit and Responsibility.* Oxford, 1960.

Amandry, P. "Eschyle et la purification d'Oreste," *Revue Archaeologique,* sixth series, XI (1938), 19-27.

Anderson, F. M. B. "The Character of Clytemnestra in the *Choephoroe* and the *Eumenides* of Aeschylus," *American Journal of Philology,* LIII (1932), 301-19.

Bernays, Jacob. *Grundzüge der verlorenen Abhandlung des Aristoteles über die Wirkung der Tragodie.* Breslau, 1857.

————. *Zwei Abhandlungen über die Aristotelische Theories des Dramas.* Berlin, 1880.

Bethe, Erich. *Homer, Dichtung und Sage.* Vol. I. Leipzig, 1914.

Bodkin, Maude. *The Quest for Salvation in an Ancient and a Modern Play.* London, 1941.

Bonner, Robert J., and Gertrude Smith. *The Administration of Justice from Homer to Aristotle.* 2 vols. Chicago, 1930, 1938.

Browder, Jonathan Bayley. "The Time Elements of the Orestean Trilogy," *Bulletin of the University of Wisconsin,* "Philology and Literature Series," Vol. II, No. 62 (1902-1903).

Bultmann, Rudolf. *Primitive Christianity in Its Contemporary Setting.* New York, 1956.

Butcher, S. H. *Aristotle's Theory of Poetry and Fine Art.* New York, 1951.

Callahan, Virginia Woods. *Types of Rulers in the Plays of Aeschylus.* Dissertation, University of Chicago, 1944.

Cherniss, Harold. *Aristotle's Criticism of Plato and the Academy.* Vol. I. Baltimore, 1944.

————. "On Plato's *Republic* X 597b," *American Journal of Philology,* LIII (1932), 233-42.

————. "Parmenides and the *Parmenides* of Plato," *American Journal of Philology,* LIII (1932), 122-38.

Chu Kwang-Tsien. *The Psychology of Tragedy.* Strasbourg, 1933.

Cooper, Lane, and A. Gudeman. "A Bibliography of the *Poetics* of Aristotle," *Cornell Studies in English,* XI (1928).

Cornford, F. M. *Plato's Cosmology.* "Library of Liberal Arts," No. 101. New York, 1957.

————. *Plato's Theory of Knowledge.* "Library of Liberal Arts," No. 100. New York, 1957.

de Coulanges, Fustel. *The Ancient* City. New York, 1955.

Croissant, Jeanne. *Aristote et les mystères.* "Bibliothèque de la faculté de philosophie et lettres de l'université de Liège," No. 51 (1942).

Daube, Benjamin. *Zu den Rechtsproblemen in Aischylos' Agamemnon.* Dissertation, Freiburg im Breisgau, 1939.

Davreux, Juliette. *La légende de la prophetesse Cassandre d'après les textes et les monuments.* "Bibliothèque de la faculté de philosophie et lettres de l'université de Liège," No. 94 (1942).

Delatte, A. *Les conceptions de l'enthousiasme chez les philosophes présocratique.* Paris, 1934.

DeWitt, N. W. "The Meaning of Katharsis in Aristotle's Definition of Tragedy," *Transactions of the Royal Society of Canada* (1934), 109-15.

Diès, A. *Autour de Platon.* 2 vols. Paris, 1927.

Dirlmeier, F. "Katharsis Pathematon," *Hermes,* LXXV (1940), 81-92.

Dodds, E. R. *The Greeks and the Irrational.* Berkeley, 1951.

Dumortier, Jean. *Les images dans la poésie d'Eschyle.* Paris, 1935.

————. *Le vocabulaire médical d'Eschyle.* Paris, 1935.

Edelstein, E. J. and L. *Asclepius: A Collection and Interpretation of the Testimonies.* 2 vols. Baltimore, 1945.

Ehrenberg, Victor. *The Greek State.* New York, 1960.

Else, G. F. "Aristotle on the Beauty of Tragedy," *Harvard Studies in Classical Philology,* XLIX (1938), 179-204.

————. *Aristotle's Poetics: The Argument.* Cambridge, Mass., 1957.

————. "A Survey of Works on Aristotle's *Poetics,*" *Classical Weekly,* XLVIII, No. 6 (1955).

Farnell, Lewis Richard. *Greek Hero Cults and Ideas of Immortality.* Oxford, 1921.

de Faye, Eugene. *Etude sur les idées religieuses et morales d'Eschyle.* Laigle, 1884.

Finley, J. H. *Pindar and Aeschylus.* "Martin Classical Lectures," Vol. XIV. Cambridge, 1955.

Flashar, Hellmut. "Die medizinischen Grundlagen der Lehre von der Wirkung der Dichtung in der griechischen Poetik," *Hermes,* LXXXIV (1956), 12-48.

Forbes, P. B. R. "Law and Politics in the Oresteia," *Classical Review,* LXII (1948), 99ff.

Freeman, Kathleen. *The Pre-Socratic Philosophers.* 3rd edition. Oxford, 1953.

Gernet, Louis. Introduction to *Les lois.* Vol. XI, Pt. I, *Platon, oeuvres complètes.* Paris, 1951.

Glanville, I. M. "Tragic Error," *Classical Quarterly,* XLIII (1949), 47-56.

Glotz, G. *La solidarité de la famille dans le droit criminel en Grèce.* Paris, 1904.

Goldman, Hetty. "The *Oresteia* of Aeschylus as Illustrated by Greek Vase Painting," *Harvard Studies in Classical Philology,* XXI (1910), 111-59.

Grand, Yvonne. *Recherche des principes d'une philosophie des arts dits d'imitation chez Platon, Aristote et Plotin.* Dissertation, Université de Fribourg, Switzerland, 1952.

Graves, Robert, *The Greek Myths.* 2 vols. Baltimore, 1955.

Greene, William Chase. *Moira.* Cambridge, Mass., 1944.

————. "The Greek Criticism of Poetry," in H. A. Levin (ed.), *Perspectives of Criticism.* Cambridge, Mass., 1950.

van Groningen, B. A. "Deux particularités de la définition aristo-
telicienne de la tragédie," *Annuaire de l'institut de philologie
et d'histoire orientales et slaves,* V (1937), 457-61.

Gudeman, Alfred. *Aristoteles Poetik.* Berlin and Leipzig, 1934.

————. "The Source of Aristotle's *Poetics,*" in *Classical Studies in
Honor of J. C. Rolfe* (1931).

Guéroult, M. "Le Xe livre des Lois et la dernière forme de la
physique platonicienne," *Revue des études grecques,* XXXVII
(1924), 27-78.

Guthrie, W. K. C. *Orpheus and Greek Religion.* London, 1935.

————. *The Greeks and Their Gods.* London, 1950.

Hafner, German. *Iudicium Orestis, Klassisches und Klassizisti-
sches.* "Winkelmannsprogramm," No. 113. Berlin, 1958.

Harris, Rendel. *The Ascent of Olympus.* Manchester, 1917.

Harrison, Jane. *Prolegomena to the Study of Greek Religion.* 3rd
edition. Cambridge, England, 1922.

————. *Themis, A Study of the Social Origins of Greek Religion.*
2nd edition. Cambridge, England, 1927.

Hathaway, Baxter. "Catharsis," in Joseph T. Shipley (ed.), *Dictionary of World Literature.* New York, 1943.

Hegel, G. F. W. *The Philosophy of Fine Art,* tr. F. P. B. Osmaston. 4 vols. London, 1920.

Henn, T. R. *The Harvest of Tragedy.* London, 1957.

Herington, C. J. *Athena Parthenos and Athena Polias.* Manchester, 1955.

Herrick, M. T. "A Supplement to Cooper and Gudeman's Bibliography of the *Poetics* of Aristotle," *American Journal of Philology,* LII (1931), 168-74.

Hignett, C. *A History of the Athenian Constitution to the End of
the 5th Century B.C.* Oxford, 1952.

House, Humphrey. *Aristotle's Poetics.* London, 1956.

Howald, E. "Ein vorplatonische Kunsttheorie," *Hermes,* LIV
(1919), 187-207.

Jacoby, Felix. *Atthis, The Local Chronicles of Ancient Athens.*
Oxford, 1949.

Jones, J. Walter. *The Law and Legal Theory of the Greeks.* Oxford, 1956.

Kitto, H. D. F. *Form and Meaning in Drama.* London, 1956.

————. *Greek Tragedy.* Garden City, 1954.

Kommerell, Max. *Lessing und Aristoteles*. Frankfurt-am-Main, 1940.

Kuhn, Helmut. "Greek Tragedy and Plato," *Harvard Studies in Classical Philology*, LII (1941), 1-40; LIII (1942), 37-88.

Lesky, Albin. "Die Orestie des Aischylos," *Hermes*, LXVI (1931), 190-214.

Lucas, F. L. *Tragedy*. London, 1928.

McMahon, A. Philip. "Seven Questions on Aristotelian Definitions of Tragedy and Comedy," *Harvard Studies in Classical Philology*, XL (1929), 97-198.

Marinatos, Spyridon. *Kreta und das mykenische Hellas*. Munich, 1959.

Méautis, Georges. *Eschyle et la trilogie*. Paris, 1936.

————. "L'Oedipe à Colone et le culte des héros," *Recueil de travaux publiés par la faculté des lettres*, No. 19. Neuchâtel, 1940.

Morrow, Glenn R. "Plato and the Rule of Law," *Philosophical Review*, L (1941), 105-26.

————. "Plato's Law of Slavery in Its Relation to Greek Law," *Illinois Studies in Language and Literature*, XXV, No. 3 (1939).

Moulinier, Louis. *Le pur et l'impur dans la pensée des Grecs; d'Homère à Aristote*. Paris, 1952.

Myers, Margaret J. "The Meaning of Katharsis," *Sewanee Review*, XXXIV (1926), 278-90.

Nilsson, Martin P. *Cults, Myths, Oracles and Politics in Ancient Greece*, "Skrifter Utgivna Av Svenska Institutet I Athen," VIII, No. 1. Lund, 1951.

————. *Greek Popular Religion*. New York, 1940.

————. *The Mycenaean Origin of Greek Mythology*. Berkeley, 1932.

Oliver, James H. *The Athenian Expounders of the Sacred and Ancestral Law*. Baltimore, 1950.

Onians, Richard Broxton. *The Origins of European Thought*. 2nd edition. Cambridge, 1954.

Owen, E. T. *The Harmony of Aeschylus*. Toronto, 1952.

Papanoutsos, E. R. *La catharsis des passions d'après Aristote*. Athens, 1953.

Pohlenz, Max. "Furcht und Mitleid?" *Hermes*, LXXXIV (1956), 49-74.

Post, L. A. *From Homer to Menander.* "Sather Classical Lectures," Vol. XXIII. Berkeley, 1951.

Quinton, A. M. "Tragedy," *The Aristotelian Society,* Suppl. Vol., XXXIV (1960), 145-64.

Ramnoux, Clémence. *La nuit et les enfants de la nuit.* Paris, 1959.

Raphael, D. D. *The Paradox of Tragedy.* Bloomington, 1960.

Reeves, Charles H. "The Aristotelian Concept of the Tragic Hero," *American Journal of Philology,* LXXIII (1952), 172-88.

Reinhardt, Karl. *Aischylos als Regisseur und Theologe.* Berne, 1949.

Reverdin, Olivier. *La religion de la cité platonicienne.* Dissertation, Université de Genève. Paris, 1945.

Ridgeway, William. "The True Scene of the Second Act of the *Eumenides* of Aeschylus," *Classical Review,* XXI (1907), 163-68.

de Romilly, J. *La crainte et l'angoise dans le théatre d'Eschyle.* Paris, 1958.

Rose, H. J. "Aeschylus the Psychologist," *Symbolae Osloenses,* No. 32 (1956), 1-21.

————. *A Commentary on the Surviving Plays of Aeschylus.* 2 vols. Amsterdam, 1958.

————. "Ghost Ritual in Aeschylus," *Harvard Theological Review,* XLIII (1950), 257-80.

————. "Theology and Mythology in Aeschylus," *Harvard Theological Review,* XXXIX (1946), 1-24.

Schaerer, René. "La composante dialectique de l'Orestie," *Revue de metaphysique et de morale,* LVIII (1953), 47-79.

Sen-Gupta, Nares Chandra. *The Evolution of Law.* 2nd revised edition. Calcutta, 1951.

Skemp, J. B. *The Theory of Motion in Plato's Later Dialogues.* Cambridge, 1942.

Snell, Bruno. "Aischylos und das Handeln im Drama," *Philologus,* Supplement Band XX, Heft 1 (Leipzig, 1928).

————. *The Discovery of the Mind,* tr. T. G. Rosenmeyer. Cambridge, Mass., 1953.

Solmsen, Friedrich. *Hesoid and Aeschylus.* "Cornell Studies in Classical Philology." Vol. XXX. Ithaca, 1949.

————. *Plato's Theology.* "Cornell Studies in Classical Philology." Vol. XXVII. Ithaca, 1942.

————. "Strata of Greek Religion in Aeschylus," *Harvard Theological Review,* XL (1940), 211-26.

————. "Tissues and the Soul," *Philosophical Review*, LIX (1950), 435-68.

Tate, J. "Imitation in Plato's *Republic*," *Classical Quarterly*, XXII (1928), 16-23.

————. "On Plato: *Laws* X 889cd," *Classical Quarterly*, XXX (1936), 48-54.

————. "Plato and Didacticism," *Hermathena*, XLVIII (1933), 93-113.

————. "Plato and 'Imitation,'" *Classical Quarterly*, XXVI (1932), 161-69.

Te Riele, Gerrit Jan Marie Jozef. *Les femmes chez Eschyle*. Djakarta, 1955.

Thier, M. *Die Kassandra des Aischylos*. Dissertation, Tübingen, 1951.

Thomson, George. *Aeschylus and Athens*. London, 1941.

Toutain, J. "L'évolution de la conception des Erinyes dans le mythe d'Oreste d'Eschyle à Euripide," in *Mélanges F. Cumont*. Brussels, 1936.

Tracy, H. L. "Aristotle on Aesthetic Pleasure," *Classical Philology*, XLI (1946), 43-46, 193-206.

Trench, W. F. "Mimesis in Aristotle's *Poetics*," *Hermathena*, XLVIII (1933), 1-24.

————. "The Function of Poetry According to Aristotle," *Studies*, XIX (1930), 549-63.

Treston, Hubert J. *Poine, a Study in Ancient Greek Blood Vengeance*. London, 1923.

Twining, Thomas. *Aristotle's Treatise on Poetry*. London, 1789.

Vanhoutte, Maurice. *La philosophie politique de Platon dans les "Lois."* Louvain, 1954.

Verdenius, W. J. *Mimesis: Plato's Doctrine of Artistic Imitation and Its Meaning to Us*. Leiden, 1949.

Vian, F. "Le conflit entre Zeus et la destinée dans Eschyle," *Revue des études grecques*, LV (1942), 190-216.

Vicaire, Paul. *Platon, critique littéraire*. Paris, 1960.

Vlastos, G. "Religion and Medicine in the Cult of Asclepius," *Review of Religion*, XIII (1949), 269-90.

Volkmann-Schluck, K. "Die Lehre von der Katharsis in der Poetik des Aristoteles," *Varia Variorum* (1952), 104-17.

Wade-Gery, H. T. "Eupatridai, Archons, and Areopagus," *Classical Quarterly*, XXV (1931), 1-11, 77-89.

————. "Studies in the Structure of Attic Society: I. Demotion-idai," *Classical Quarterly*, XXV (1931), 129-43.

————. "Studies in the Structure of Attic Society: II. The Laws of Kleisthenes," *Classical Quarterly*, XXVII (1933), 17-29.

Webster, T. B. L. "Fourth Century Thought and the *Poetics*," *Hermes*, LXXXII (1954), 294-308.

————. *From Mycenae to Homer*. London, 1958.

————. "Plato and Aristotle as Critics of Greek Art," *Symbolae Osloenses*, XXIX (1952), 8-23.

————. "Political Interpretations in Greek Literature," *Publications of the University of Manchester*, "Classical Series," No. 6 (1948).

Weil, H. *Étude sur le drame antique*. Paris, 1897.

Wheelwright, Philip. *The Burning Fountain*. Bloomington, 1954.

Winnington-Ingram, R. P. "Aeschylus, *Agamemnon* 1343-71," *Classical Quarterly*, N.S. IV (1954), 23-30.

————. "A Religious Function of Greek Tragedy," *Journal of Hellenic Studies*, LXXIV (1954), 16-24.

————. "Clytemnestra and the Vote of Athena," *Journal of Hellenic Studies*, LXVIII (1948), 130-47.

————. "The Role of Apollo in the *Oresteia*," *Classical Review*, XLVII (1933), 97-104.

Wolff, Hans Julius. "Marriage Law and Family Organization in Ancient Athens," *Traditio*, II (1944), 43-95.

INDEX

INDEX

Aegisthus, 11n, 83-84
Aeschylus, 100-1, 130
  deity, conception of, 68
  drama, conception of, 66-67
  as dramatic artist, 95-97
  dramatic characters, treatment of, 6n, 96-97
  Erinyes, depiction of, 53
  law and religion, relationship of, 79-97
  philosophical concerns, 7-8
  and Plato, 29-30, 64-65, 85-88
  self-control, concern with, 117
Agamemnon, 16, 83
Agamemnon, 12, 30, 34
Althea, 12
Amazons, 66
Apollo, 12, 13, 17, 19-21, 31, 56, 59-60, 63, 65, 67, 117
  Erinyes, dispute with, 41-45
  miasma and catharsis, interest in, 49-52, 97
  on superiority of male, 45, 68-70
Aquinas, 91
Areopagus, 141
  and Erinyes, 54
  founded by Athena, 66, 76
Argos, 14, 79, 83, 142
Aristotle, 99, 105, 115-16, 123, 127, 130
  catharsis, interpretation of, 10, 103 and *passim*
  on enthusiasm and melancholia, 118-19, 120-21
  good man, conception of, 131-32
  on imitation, 133-36
  on reproduction, 47
  Athenian Constitution, 76
  De Anima, 120, 124-25

  Metaphysics, 125, 131
  Nicomachean Ethics, 137
  On the Generation of Animals, 46-47
  Organon, 77
  Physics, 130-31
  Poetics, 101 and *passim*
  Politics, 74, 121-22
  Rhetoric, 128-29
Art
  as imitation, 122
  in its moral function, 10
Artist, 100-1
  special knowledge of, 131-33
  as technician, 131
Asclepius, 12, 18, 19, 20
Athena, 9, 12, 13, 14, 21, 36, 52, 56, 63, 65-67, 84, 88, 97, 141
  and Erinyes, 67-72, 75-76, 82
Athens, 14, 29, 67, 79, 99, 100
Atreus, 30, 59

Bernays, J., 104
Bethe, E., 41
Butcher, S. H., 106
Bywater, I., 106

Callahan, V. W., 83
Cassandra, 40-41
Catharsis, 97, 103 and *passim*
  as aesthetic concept, 111-13
  as cognitive concept, 107-11, 119
  as medical concept, 105-7
  as religious concept, 113-15
  in *Oedipus Rex*, 138-41
  in *Oresteia*, 138-41
Chaos, 71n
Character, development of in Greek drama, 6n, 96-97